"Decades ago Phillips Plastics Corporation informally defined its culture as the People Process. Simply put '. . . all people are important and people working together achieve more . . .' Some grasp the concept, but Drs. Jeanette Black and Kelly La Venture embraced the meaning, finding people in diverse industries and businesses who share the belief that its people are a critical part of an organization's success."

—*Debbie Cervenka*, Executive Vice President (former),
Phillips Plastics Corporation

"The authors of *The Human Factor to Profitability* have scored a winner with this book that finally brings to the forefront how profitability doesn't happen through osmosis. Rather, it's a careful mix of creating a culture where people are the most significant catalysts to profitability. While many organizations give lip service to this mantra, *The Human Factor to Profitability* provides concrete strategies for creating a people-process culture. Rich with examples, inclusive of top leadership thinkers, and robust with evidence-based practices, this book provides a clear road map to achieving profitability through people-process initiatives. Whether you are a CEO, HR professional, organization development consultant, or business manager, this book is a must read from the first page to the last."

—*Dr. Mitchell Kusy*, Professor, Antioch University, Corporate Psychologist,
Co-author, *Toxic Workplace! Managing Toxic
Personalities and Their Systems of Power*

"With the publication of *The Human Factor to Profitability: Building a People-Centered Culture for Long-Term Success*, Drs. Black and La Venture have written the must-read text of the year for all of us—consultants, academicians, business leaders, and students—who work each day to keep the and between people and profits."

—*Dr. Diane B. Stoy*

"This book captures the essence of what it takes to build and sustain a High-Performance Organization. Drs. Black and La Venture delved into the history to glean the insight on the impact and effectiveness of corporate cultures. The authors identify several elements needed to create a high-performing, people-centered culture. One of those is trust. This cannot be overstated. Many in authority fail to become leaders mainly, because they lack the trust of the people they are supposed to lead. Implementing the concepts and insights gained from this book will help you transform your organization."

—*Dr. Raj Beekie,* Adjunct Professor

WITH A FOREWORD BY KAT LUI, PHD,
AND DEBBIE CERVENKA

THE
HUMAN
FACTOR
TO
Profitability

Building *a* **People-Centered** Culture
for Long-Term Success

· · · · ·

Jeanette Black, EdD, SPHR, *and*
Kelly La Venture, EdD

RIVER GROVE
BOOKS

This Research has been approved by the UW–Stout IRB as required by the Code of Federal Regulations Title 45 Part 46.

Published by River Grove Books
Austin, TX
www.rivergrovebooks.com

Distributed by River Grove Books

Design and composition by Greenleaf Book Group
Cover design by Greenleaf Book Group
Kelly La Venture's author photo by Bob Gross

Cataloging-in-Publication data is available.

Print ISBN: 978-1-63299-054-9

eBook ISBN: 978-1-63299-055-6
First Edition

Contents

Foreword

In 1964, a small, group of manufacturing pioneers helped a new plastics firm make its first part—a white calendar frame—in an abandoned creamery in rural Wisconsin. Cramped for space, short on cash, but big on dreams, they unknowingly started on a journey that would lead to one of America's great manufacturing success stories: Phillips Plastics Corporation. Along the way, they discovered that all people have intrinsic worth and value and deserve to be treated with dignity and respect. From this core belief, a high-performance organizational culture evolved that focused on people as the key to individual, business, and community success. Called the people process, this underlying value system served as the company's foundation, supporting business structure, strategies, and tactics. For Bob Cervenka, cofounder of Phillips, making long-term investments in people and communities yielded more than financial dividends. Quite simply, it was the right thing to do. As Debbie Cervenka, vice president of marketing stated, "The impact a people-centered culture has on the workforce—and the workforce means everybody from upper management to the people working on the plant floor—is directly related to a trust factor. If you share information with your people, your people can verify and understand that the information is true and honest, [if] it's given on a regular basis, openly and willingly. They [the employees] begin to trust in the organization. Trust isn't something that you can buy."

Organizations today are challenged by a war for talent. An organization's culture is considered part of its competitive advantage for attracting and retaining that talent. In people-centered cultures, the employees are the primary attribute of the organization, and organizations develop business processes around and in concert with employees as the central concept. As a result, healthy workplaces are formed that focus on employee well-being, information sharing, and communication, which results in improved organizational performance.

In describing this type of workplace, Debbie Cervenka said, "What really made a difference was when you share information, you take down walls and barriers in an organization. So you know whether the company is doing well. If it isn't doing well, why [isn't it]? So if you communicate that to people and they see that, at the end of the year, they see you're having a two-percent bonus instead of a six-percent bonus, they know why. They know that it's an investment in the future. They know that every person is going to benefit. Second, we chose to compensate people for talent in their base salary. But, collectively, when you run your organization, valuing all people [and] respecting all people, you find that those people take ownership and pride, and the end result becomes meaningful. Because we built the best products, . . . our sales grew as a direct result of having people committed to the organization—people who wanted to excel and who didn't just want a job. They actually wanted a career and to be a part of building something."

The purpose of this book is to provide access to information, knowledge, and learning relative to this concept. It is meant for students, business leaders, human resources (HR) and talent leaders, organizational change facilitators, and anyone with an interest and passion for high-performance organizational cultures. This book provides background related to the concepts of organizational culture, organizational climate, and high-performance organizations (HPOs). Readers will also become familiar with the concepts and impact of the people-focused culture philosophy, not only as it was originally implemented at Phillips Plastics under Bob and Debbie Cervenka, the practical application illustrated by the business leaders featured in this book, and the research presented by the authors. It also presents the emerging research on the organizational structures post economic recession and how organizations are changing to successfully attract and retain employees using a people-centered approach that promotes corporate social responsibility and more sustainable organizations. This book provides tremendous insight about the impact and importance of people-centered organizational cultures in today's highly competitive global business climate.

Kat Lui, PhD, and Debbie Cervenka

Acknowledgments

Debbie Cervenka opened the doors to a new beginning and understanding of organizational life for students, faculty, and organizational members and leaders. I appreciate her support and encouragement and that of the University of Wisconsin–Stout and of our interview participants, who allowed this research to reach publication. In addition, I would like to thank the publisher, Greenleaf Book Group, for their support, resources, and commitment and belief in this subject matter. The publication and dissemination of this work will allow a refocusing on organizational culture on a global level, which will affect not only organizations but also society at large.

Jeanette Black, EdD, SPHR
Associate professor and endowed chair of
People Process Culture (2012–2015)
University of Wisconsin–Stout

. . . . .

Words can't express, even a fraction of, my gratitude to Bob and Debbie Cervenka for their inspiration and support. I know I speak for all those who came in contact with this wonderful couple when I say that their management philosophy is opening doors for educators and practitioners to implement changes in the way organizations are concerned with their people. My gratitude also extends to my son Ryley and our family for endless patience and inspiration.

Dr. Kelly La Venture, Assistant
Professor, Bemidji State University

CHAPTER 1

People-Process Culture

As stated in the Foreword, the people process culture recognizes that all people have intrinsic worth and deserve to be treated with respect. In 1964, Phillips Plastics Corporation paved the way for a high-performance organizational culture that recognized these values. The leadership at Phillips Plastics placed emphasis on character, teamwork, and extraordinarily high ethical standards, from which a unique organizational culture evolved in which business was viewed as a moral enterprise, as well as a profit-generating one.

Bob Cervenka, cofounder of Phillips Plastics Corporation, firmly believed that it was important to make long-term investments in people and the community to yield even greater financial dividends. He stated, "Morality in business, the integrity of having a moral culture, should never be compromised." He also fervently believed in open communications and sharing the wealth with people through profit sharing and a team-based incentive plan. "The *what's mine is mine, what's yours is half mine* philosophy of many businesses hurts too many people" (Original PPC Handbook, Phillips Plastics Corporation, 1994).

Leslie Lagerstrom, former vice president of marketing of Phillips Plastics Corporation, fondly remembered the impact that Bob had on the organization. "The people-process culture was strongest in the building that Bob resided in—it glowed the brightest there" (L. Lagerstrom, personal communication, June 26, 2014).

Organizational Culture

Organizational culture is a collective experience that emerges from the beliefs and social interactions of its members (Schneider, Brief, & Guzzo, 1996; Trice & Beyer, 1993). These interactions contain shared values, mutual understandings, patterns of beliefs, and expectations of behavior that are created over time within an organization (Schein, 2004). Organizational culture also distinguishes members from one organization to another, which provides a sense of identity (Alvesson, 2011).

Table 1-1. Definitions of Organizational Culture

Author	Definition
Kroeber & Kluckhohn (1952)	Transmitted patterns of values, ideas, and other symbolic systems that shape behavior of an organization.
Hofstede (1980)	The collective programming of the mind that distinguishes the members of the organization from another. This included shared beliefs, values and practices that distinguished one organization to another.
Swartz & Jordon (1980)	Patterns of beliefs and expectations shared by members that produce norms shaping behavior.
Ouchi (1981)	Set of symbols, ceremonies, and myths that communicate the underlying values and beliefs of the organization to its employees.
Martin & Siehl (1983)	Glue that holds together an organization through shared patterns of meaning. Three component systems: context or core values, forms/process of communication (e.g., jargon), strategies to reinforce content (e.g., rewards, training programs).
Uttal (1983)	Shared values (what is important) and beliefs (how things work) that interact with organization's structures and control systems to produce behavioral norms (the way we do things around here).
Adler (1986)	Refers to something shared by all or almost all members of some social groups, something that the older members of the group try to pass on to the younger members, and something that shapes organizational behavior or structure.

Continued

Author	Definition
Denison (1990)	Refers to the underlying values, beliefs, and principles that serve as a foundation for an organization's management system as well as the set of management practices and behaviors that both exemplify and reinforce those basic principles.
Schein (1992, 2004, 2010)	A pattern of shared basic assumptions learned by a group as it evolved its problems of external adaptation and internal integration, which has worked well enough to be considered valid and, therefore to be taught to new members as the correct way to perceive, think, and feel in relation to those problems.
Trompenaars (1993)	The way in which people solve problems. It is a shared system of meanings. It dictates what we pay attention to, how we act, and what we value.
Goffee (1996)	Is an outcome of how people relate to one another.
Schnieder (1997)	Shared patterns of behavior and the meaning of that behavior.
Cameron & Quinn (1999)	What is valued, the dominant leadership styles, the language of success that makes an organization unique.
Sullivan (2001)	Refers to the total lifestyle of a people, including all the values, ideas, knowledge, behaviors, and material objects that they share.
Wood (2001)	The systems of shared beliefs and values that develop within an organization or within its subunits that guides the behaviors of its members.
Wiesner (2002)	A way of looking at organizations by its shared values and behavior.
Thomas & Tung (2003)	Refers to evolving set of shared beliefs, values, attitudes, and logical processes that provide cognitive maps for people within a given societal group to perceive, think, reason, act, react, and interact.
Anthon (2004)	The set of values, beliefs, and understanding shared by an organization's employees and its rank among an organization's most powerful component.
Taylor (2004)	Refers to what is created from the messages that are received about how people are expected to behave in the organization.
Wagner (2005)	An informal, shared way of perceiving life and membership in the organization that binds members together and influences what they think about themselves and their work.
Hofstede (2005)	The unwritten book with rules of the social game.

Source: Adapted from *Culture, Leadership, and Organizations: The GLOBE Study of 62 Societies*, by R. J. House, P. J. Hanges, M. Javidan, P. W. Dorfman, and V. Gupta, 2004, Thousand Oaks, CA: Sage (as cited in Abu-Jarad, I. Y., Yusof, N., & Nikbin, D. (2010). A review paper on organizational culture and organizational performance. *International Journal of Business and Social Science 1*(3), p. 35.) Copyright 2004 by Sage. Adapted with permission.

There are many definitions and perspectives about organizational culture (Table 1-1). As a result, organizations can be viewed as dynamic interactive components that possess a sense of energy from the interactions between individuals and the commonality of shared values (Schein, 2010). Organizational culture, when it is rooted in shared values and a deep sense of purpose that people find meaningful, serves as a powerful framework and filter for making decisions at all levels within an organization. Culture provides the unwritten rules of the workplace. These rules are those expected behaviors, such as codes of conduct and dress codes, that provide structure within the organization. Table 1-2 provides an overview of selected frameworks that adhere to these various definitions and their specific components related to organizational culture.

Table 1-2. Models and Components of a High-Performance Organization

	Characteristics

Author: Schein (2010) **Framework:** 3 Levels of Organizational Culture	1. Artifacts
	 • Visible and feel-able structures and processes
	 • Observed behavior
	  • Difficult to decipher
	2. Espoused beliefs and values
	 • Ideas, goals, values, aspirations
	 • Ideologies
	 • Rationalizations
	  • May or may not be congruent with behavior and other artifacts
	3. Basic underlying assumptions
	 • Unconscious, taken-for-granted beliefs and values
	  • Determine behavior, perception, thought and feeling

Continued

	Characteristics

Author:
Cameron and Quinn (1999)
 	
Framework:
Competing Values Framework
	Four culture types divided into quadrants based on flexibility versus stability and internal versus external focus:
	1. Clan
	  • Family oriented
	  • Friendly place to work
	  • Leaders considered as mentors
	  • Leaders as "parent" figures
	  • Loyalty and tradition
	  • Importance of cohesion and morale
	  • Success defined by sensitivity to customers and concern for people
	  • High focus on teamwork, participation and consensus
	2. Adhocracy
	  • Dynamic entrepreneurial environment
	  • Creativity encouraged and valued
	  • Innovative and risk taking
	  • Commitment to experimentation and innovation
	  • Being the leader on products and technology valued
	  • Long-term emphasis on growth and acquisition of new resources
	  • Success is gaining new products and services
	  • Encourages individual initiative and freedom
	3. Hierarchy
	  • Formal structure
	  • Policies and procedures govern work
	  • Leaders are good coordinators and organizers
	  • Smooth running organization is valued
	  • Efficiency
	  • Long-term focus on stability and performance
	  • Success defined in terms of dependable delivery, smooth scheduling and low cost
	  • Job security and predictability
	4. Market
	  • Results oriented
	  • Focus on getting the work done
	  • Competitive and goal oriented
	  • Leaders drive for results
	  • Emphasis on winning
	  • Reputation and success
	  • Focus on achievement and measurable goals
	  • Success defined in terms of market share and penetration
	  • Competitive pricing and market leadership are important
	  • Competitive organizational style

Continued

	Characteristics
Author: Cardador and Rupp (2011) **Framework:** Organizational culture, multiple needs, and meaningfulness of work framework	Focus on culture type, need fulfillment, and meaningfulness 1. Innovative Culture • Entrepreneurial, personal initiative, and growth • Employee management focus is in risk taking, innovation, freedom, and uniqueness • Leadership style is entrepreneurial, innovator, and visionary 2. Supportive Culture • Employee empowerment, humane work environment • Employee management focus on teamwork, participation, and consensus • Leadership style is facilitator, mentor, and parental focused 3. Market • Competitiveness, productivity, and profit oriented • Approach to managing employees is demanding, fostering competition • Hard driving, competitive, production based leadership style 4. Bureaucratic • Efficiency, stability and productivity valued • Control, conformity, and stability • Organization, monitoring, rules, and structured style of leadership Fulfillment needs are aligned based on • Need for control • Need for belongingness • Need for meaningful existence Sources of meaningfulness are derived from • Meaningful tasks • Meaningful relationships • Meaningful goals and values The needs are interpreted based on their "perceived meaningfulness." Boundary conditions determine outcomes: • Cultural consistency • Combined cultures • Ethical culture • Individual differences

Continued

	Characteristics
Author: Keyton (2011)	Organizational culture revealed through a series of organizational lenses
Framework: Organizational Lens Framework	1. Symbolic Performance • Symbols (objects, words, or actions)—including the everyday and unique—that are used in the organization and stand for something else 2. Narrative Reproduction • Stories told by organizational members 3. Textual Reproduction • Formal organizational documents; informal employee electronic documents 4. Management • Treating organizational culture as a managerial resource or tool; an internal process that influences organizational outcomes 5. Power and Politics • Revelation of organizational ideology, especially organizational values about employees 6. Technology • Organizational use of technology required to accomplish its mission; use of technology to control employees 7. Globalization • Intersection of organizational culture and national culture

Organizational culture can appear transparent or even nonexistent to those embedded in the culture. This general acceptance of the culture reflects the deeply held beliefs and behavior norms of the group, which is frequently referred to as the organization's soul or its organizational glue—what holds its disparate pieces (the employees) together. It is often only when someone new joins the group that the unspoken expectations for practices or decision-making processes—how things are done around here—surface (Schein, 2010). Culture manifests in various ways, because employees bring different interests, experiences, responsibilities, and values with them into the organization (Martin, 2005), and culture is interpreted, evaluated, and enacted on the basis of these unique employee views. Practices within the culture that indicate what is perceived as right or wrong, good or bad, define that culture (Gehman & Trevino, 2013).

The importance of organizational culture cannot be overstated. In this book, we advocate a culture built around people—the employees, management, and leadership. This is the human factor of profitability. A people-focused approach has been proven to lead to long-term, lasting success.

The Tenets of the People-Process Culture

Traditionally, the dilemma of the CEO has been described as balancing shareholder demands with achieving longevity or sustainability. Perhaps the dilemma should be rewritten as providing an environment that espouses individual freedom while ensuring that the financial and nonfinancial targets of the organization are met. Individual freedom provides the basis for creativity, innovation, and building trust between individuals. However, the organization and the senior executives need to shift their focus from numbers and results to the establishment of an environment designed to build trust to maintain the appropriate performance measures that are acceptable to its staff (Weymes, 2005). Following these core principles allows people-process organizations to consistently perform at exceptional levels over an extended period of time.

Tom Walter stated his belief that he and his leadership team "are here to grow our people, not use our people. We are here to motivate our people, not manipulate our people. Our people are . . . our most . . . valuable asset" (T. Walter, personal communication, July 15, 2014).

Walter also shared how he creates a sustainable, employee-centered culture. "Our short-term objectives are to create behaviors that embrace our employee-centered culture. . . . Then the people of the organization make it successful. So if you are looking for affordable, sustainable culture, you are looking to align with a people-process culture. . . . The short term is to set that system of behaviors within the staff that will lead to evolving a continuous change model and create sustainability. . . . It is not just about one personality or one dynamic; it is about how the organization grows . . . to create that behavior and embrace that design of employee culture, leading to sustainability. . . . If we hire the right people and provide them the right culture, they will have the antecedents and the behaviors [to achieve high performance]" (T. Walter, personal communication, July 15, 2014).

People-process cultures are founded on the ideas that

- all people are important,
- a strong belief in people shapes the organizational culture,
- happy people working together perform at higher levels, and
- all people benefit as a result.

All People Are Important

The view that all people are important provides the foundation for creating an exciting, supportive, dynamic, and innovative work environment. It also supports substantial growth and profits. To accomplish this, organizational leaders, middle management, and frontline supervisors shift their focus from numbers and results to the organization's greatest asset—its employees. When the corporate environment is designed to focus on its people, it builds trust, leverages the talent within the organization, and can be used to develop performance measures and business success factors that are reflective of the employee culture.

Lawler (as cited in Weymes, 2005) listed six characteristics that can be used to describe high performance in people-centered organizations, a focus on individual involvement, effective leadership, and moving away from systems and processes as the basis for control:

- Organizational cultures can be the ultimate competitive advantage.
- Involvement can be the most effective source of control.
- All employees add significant value.
- Lateral processes are the key to organizational efficiencies.
- Organizations should be designed around people, products, and customers.
- Efficient leadership that is focused on employees is the key to organizational leadership.

As a result, workers feel that they get to do what they do best—every day, that their opinions count, that their coworkers share their commitment to quality, and that they feel a personal connection between their work and the company's mission. The impact of the people-process culture is substantial and synergistic (Weymes, 2005).

According to the *2014 Talent Management and Rewards Study by Towers Watson © (2014a)*, high-performance, people-focused organizations support that focus by

- reinvigorating career management strategies,
- rethinking managers' roles and equipping them to succeed, and
- reallocating and differentiating rewards to reflect the employee value proposition.

The organizational dilemma can be simply stated: The company must create an environment where trust, creativity, and innovation flourish while meeting the performance criteria specified by the stakeholders. Applying this philosophy to organization design ensures that the nature of the organization is shaped by the people in the organization. The starting point for designing, developing, and transforming an organization lies in the understanding of the people in the organization and the relationships between these individuals and external stakeholders (Weymes, 2005). Developing the vision and goals, creating a focus on the customer, and developing systems and processes are not to be ignored. The starting point lies in the nature of the relationship among people (Sagiv, Schwartz, & Arieli, 2011).

When an organization is focused on the numbers, rules, and regulations, inevitably systems and processes tend to be developed to ensure staff conformance to those rules. Such quantitative targets usually dictate behavior. Rules and regulations control behavior, stifle creativity, and build an environment based on mistrust, self-interest and ambition, deceit, and complaints. But the organization that creates an environment that allows its staff freedom may generate new and innovative approaches, foster harmonious working relationships, and build trust and integrity. Unfortunately, too many organizations use customer service, production efficiencies, and HR (learning) to control financial outcomes (Weymes, 2005).

Therefore, an organization's performance depends on the nature of the relationships formed by individuals within that organization and its relationships with external stakeholders. Employees are rational individuals who are seeking self-actualization (achieving one's purpose in life), happiness, and wisdom. However, in a bureaucratic organization, the rules and regulations are designed to control behavior, while the reward structures are designed to buy the individual's desire for the perfect life. Unfortunately, the workplace can often create a work environment where employees have little commitment to their employer and, therefore, little loyalty (Weymes, 2005). The challenge facing organizations is creating an environment where individuals can fulfill their own dreams as well as those of the organization, while respecting the social norms of society (Weymes, 2005).

The success and synergy of the people process is the foundational belief that all people—employees, customers, suppliers, and community members—are important. This belief in people and the accompanying values of treating each person and task with dignity, trust, and respect serve as both the bedrock foundation for business decisions and a springboard for performance, growth, and innovation. Thus all people benefit in the challenges, risk, and success of the organization, resulting in increased employee engagement and commitment.

"I believe the people process," said Bob Cervenka, "how people work together—how they treat each other, the values they share—is critical to business success." Such relationships are based on high levels of trust between individuals that is vested in shared values, beliefs, and attitudes.

A Strong Belief in People Shapes the Organizational Culture

Built to last, people-process cultures see their people as a long-term investment, a source of competitive advantage that must be supported and protected at all times. Conservatively financed—yet hard-hitting and aggressive—companies with people-process cultures view risk and even failure as necessary parts of growing a business. Organizations that are fixated on their financial growth or the return on investment are more focused on winning. Winning is important, but by focusing on the people of the organization, both the company and the employees win, whereas financial growth benefits only the shareholders; it does little to excite or motivate employees. The common denominator among successful high-performance organizations (HPOs) is people: Their organizational cultures are centered and dependent on people. Founded on strong organizational core values, these dynamic employee enterprises have big goals and big dreams.

Chancellor Bob Meyer of UW–Stout stated, "The university, going back to effectiveness, really is connected with the people . . . here, doing the work at every level. . . . It's the people [who] are going to make the university special. So having people first as a core value is absolutely essential. If we don't put people first, we are not going to succeed" (B. Meyer, personal communication, October 6, 2014).

Organizations grounded in people-first values, great work processes, and smart business strategies have corporate cultures free from much of the stress, strain, and bureaucratic insanity that remains prevalent in corporate life. As a result, firms with healthy people-process cultures are constantly changing and adapting to new ideas, people, resources, technology, challenges, and opportunities (Sagiv et al., 2011).

Happy People Working Together Perform at Higher Levels

In today's fast-paced business environment, the quality of working relationships and trust generated by unwavering business integrity is emerging as a key competitive and strategic advantage. (Sagiv et al., 2011) showed that people-focused cultures, coupled with effective leadership, help managers respond more rapidly to customer needs and changes in the business environment. Because leadership and frontline managers care deeply about their people, they tend to listen more intently to what the company's various stakeholders have to say (Sagiv et al., 2011). Adaptive organizations consistently and substantially outperform companies with more traditional corporate cultures on four major measures: revenue, workforce expansion, stock price, and net income.

Tom Walter strives to create a harmonious work environment for his employees. In our 2014 interview, he stated, "So our job in the people-process culture system is to remove the disruptors from the people's lives by using the culture. Then the people are happy. Our staff is happy. Their engagement increases. Their discretionary thinking becomes positive instead of negative. That whole process of [a people-centered culture] works magnificently, if it's used" (T. Walter, personal communication, July 15, 2014).

Employees depend on the company, and companies depend on their employees; no firm can be successful without manpower to perform their services. The primary things people bring to the workforce are talent, knowledge, ideas, and perception. People-process managers and their team members are often the first to recognize new and emerging opportunities, processes, and technologies.

Organizational culture is made up of the shared minds and values of the individuals in that organization and, therefore, connects the personal and the organizational levels. Understood as the glue between people and the organization, the organizational culture provides the firm with a high level of structural stability and reliability (Freiling & Fichtner, 2010). If a worker is distraught or has internal value conflicts, the business is going to see a diminished return and a tremendous loss in the value of that employee as a contributor to the organization (Duxbury & Gover, 2011).

Jeffrey Cernohous, general manager of Stratasys AMC, says when you have a people-process culture, "people want to come to work. It's fun. They don't have to worry about this manager or that manager or politics. I mean all that happens, but it's fun, and they want to work.

They feel like they are part of a greater good" (J. Cernohous, personal communication, July 25, 2014).

Through the process of self-discovery, employees are able to determine what they are seeking in life, their ambition, their purpose—their inspirational dream (Weymes, 2005). For an organization to ensure that there is a high degree of commitment among the employees, it is necessary to make certain that a match exists between the purpose of the organization and the dreams of the individuals (Weymes, 2005). Individual inspirational dreams become the inspirational dreams of organizations. The power of the inspirational dream lies in the message it conveys, first to those in the organization and then to the external stakeholders.

All People Benefit as a Result

To have an impact on long-term economic performance, a people-first corporate culture must be embedded in the day-to-day operations of the company. When leaders at all levels truly believe that all people are important and support that belief with their actions, amazing things can happen. There is a strong correlation between a belief in people, working together, and long-term profit and growth for everyone involved.

Bob Cervenka said it best when he stated, "When each of us understands, believes, and practices [the idea] that all people are important, we, too, will also realize that people working together will achieve more. It's part of the people process."

People-process cultures are founded on a pervasive, people-first value system that influences corporate structure, decision making, and behavior. Faith in people, concern for how people are treated and for how they treat each other, and a belief in the power of teamwork are the soul-felt values that drive HPOs.

Seven Key Elements Sustain People-Process Cultures

Research by Kendall and Bodinson (2010) and Krueger (1994) suggest that people-process cultures share the following key elements:

- leveraging people-first core values,
- leadership that walks the talk,
- open communication,
- high levels of trust,
- aligned operations and work environments focused on HR and talent development practices,
- change responsiveness, and
- organizational resiliency (Kendall & Bodinson, 2010; Krueger, 1994).

These elements are incorporated into the fabric of the organization and are built on the aspirations, talents, and dreams of the employees and constantly interact with and shape each other (Kendall & Bodinson, 2010). Organizations that promote such values as openness, trust, initiative, teamwork and collaboration, the humane treatment of workers, creativity, quality, empowerment, and delegation obtain better results (Becker, Huslid, & Ulrich, 2001; Huang & Dastmalchian, 2006). Dearlove and Coomber (1999) found that organizations experienced significantly lower employee turnover when they valued respect and teamwork (Hassan, 2007).

CHAPTER 2

People-First Core Values

Research by Oakland and Oakland (2001) indicated that organizations that are identified as world class value and invest in their people through the following actions:

- strategic alignment of HR management policies,
- effective communication,
- employee empowerment and involvement,
- training and development,
- teams and teamwork, and
- review and continuous improvement.

Not surprisingly, their research showed that world-class organizations study, value, and invest in their people through an ongoing quest for effective management and through the development of their organization's personnel (Oakland & Oakland, 2001). They value people as human beings instrumental to their organization's effectiveness.

High-Performance Organizations Have People-First Core Values

HPOs value people. The people-first mentality often begins with the founder's establishment of people-first core values that are then instilled in the organization's culture and used to drive its business strategy. People-first values also add value and address concerns from employees, the economic business climate, and so on across the organization (Hill, Hill, & Thomas, 2014). If companies fail to invest in their employees, they risk jeopardizing their own success and, ultimately, their survival (Bassi & McMurrer, 2007).

HPOs are a benevolent culture in which every human being is individually valued. Ideals, principles, and morals shape our view of the world, which, in turn, creates our priorities and affects the decisions we make (Wilson & Wilson, 1998). HPOs are humane organizations in which their stakeholders are encouraged to be supportive, helpful, and interested in the suggestions and ideas of others (Cooke & Hartman, 1989). While organizational values align and balance the organization, they also hold the organization steadfast and help answer the questions, "Who are we as an organization?" and "What do we stand for?" (Sisodia, Wolfe, & Sheth, 2014).

Through their benevolent culture, HPOs embrace people-first strategies and accept that intangible assets cannot always be reflected on the corporate balance sheet (Fulmer, Gerhart, & Scott, 2003, p. 969).

Organizational Values

Organizational values are a company's foundation for governance. The more ambiguous and uncertain the environment is, the more unstable and less enduring are the organizational values to the employees, which creates distrust in the organization (Adler, 2001; Schein, 2010). Specific values practices are only as strong and durable as the social network and fabric within a culture. Such networks can be a source of resiliency or fragility, depending on the organizational environment (Gehman & Trevino, 2013). A company's success is thought to be achieved when that organization's values are focused on its people and become enduring—central to the operation—and taken for granted within it (Hartel & Ashkanasy, 2011).

Organizational culture establishes both inspiration and aspiration. It reflects the purpose of the organization and creates a sense of belonging among its members. A company's culture is the essence of the organization and dictates how the organization approaches challenges, as well as representing the beliefs and attitudes that inspire the staff (Denton, 1996). It captures not only the character of the organization but also the emotional characteristics of the individuals within the organization. It provides the firm with personality, moving it from a mechanistic and impersonal object to a living being capable of growing and transforming (Weymes, 2005).

Values are general standards or principles that are considered desirable, such as loyalty, helpfulness, fairness, predictability, reliability, honesty, responsibility, integrity, competence, consistency, and openness (Olson & Zanna, 1993; Rokeach, 1973). Typically, employees incorporate organizational values into their own value systems and prioritize them in terms of their relative importance as guiding principles (Rokeach, 1973). An employee's value system guides his or her behavior and interpretation of experience by furnishing criteria that can be used to evaluate and understand events and actions in the surrounding work environment. A value system determines which behaviors, events, situations, or people are desirable within organizations (Jones & George, 1998). Values vary not only by content but also by function or purpose. Those for conformity and routine, for example, can undermine creativity and innovation (Hultman, 2005). The visible dimension of culture is reflected in the espoused values, philosophy, and mission of the organization, whereas the invisible dimension lies in the unspoken set of values that guide employees' actions and perceptions in the organization (Martins & Meyer, 2012; McDermott & O'Dell, 2001).

Although deeply shared core values serve as the people-process foundation and lifeblood of an organization, HR and other behind-the-scenes support systems keep work groups—and the company—running smoothly. Conversely, when critical data and support are missing, business success—even if the people-first core values of the organization are respected—becomes exceedingly difficult. The need to assess values has become imperative, because globalization has made organizations such powerful institutions that their decisions affect us all (Hultman, 2005). Therefore, a people-focused organizational culture is critical.

Organizational Climate

Organizational climate, which is defined as "a set of measurable properties of the work environment, perceived directly or indirectly by the people who live and work in this environment and assumed to influence their motivation and behavior" (Litwin & Stringer, 1968, p. 1), is important in organizational development primarily because providing a good workplace for employees is a key consideration for modern organizations. Value systems are the foundation of an organization's climate, and a good workplace environment entails a strong value system that has been put into action (Momeni, 2009).

Organizational climate is studied through a variety of lenses (Keyton, 2011). Schneider (1996) summarized the vastness and the vagueness of the field as follows: "Different researchers have used the same terminology to mean different things to the extent that providing a definitive description of *climate* has been likened to nailing Jell-o to the wall" (p. 1). This divergence of definitions notwithstanding, organizational climate is a label used to describe the perceptions, temporary attitudes, and feelings of individuals in an organization (Schneider, 1996). Also, organizational climate is subtly different from organizational culture, which requires further finesse in its organization-level analysis.

There are many approaches to climate theory and proliferations of meanings regarding the definition of organizational climate. Therefore, Table 2-1 was designed to provide several popular definitions of organizational climate and the focus of the defining author's work.

Table 2-1. Definitions of Organizational Climate

Definition	Focus	Author
A set of attributes specific to a particular organization that may be induced from the way the organization deals with its members and its environment. For the individual member within an organization, climate takes on the form of a set of attitudes and expectancies, which describe the organization in terms of both static characteristics such as degree of autonomy and behavior—outcome related contingencies.	Managerial behavior, performance, and effectiveness	Campbell, Dunnette, Lawler, & Weick (1970)
Organizational climate is a set of characteristics that describe an organization and that (a) distinguish the organization from other organizations (b) are relatively enduring over time and (c) influence the behavior of people in the organization.	Environmental variations in studies of organizational behavior	Forehand & Gilmer (1964, p. 459)
A set of measurable properties of the work environment, perceived directly or indirectly by the people who live and work in this environment and assumed to influence their motivation and behavior.	Motivation and organizational climate	Litwin & Stringer (1968, p. 1)

Continued

Definition	Focus	Author
Organizational climate is a relatively enduring characteristic of an organization that distinguishes it from other organizations and (a) embodies members' collective perceptions about their organizations with respect to such dimensions as autonomy, trust, cohesiveness, support, recognition, innovation, and fairness; (b) is produced by member interactions; (c) serves as a basis for interpreting the situation; (d) reflects prevalent norms, values and attitudes of the organization's culture; and (e) acts as a source of influence for shaping behavior.	Climate and culture	Moran & Volkwein (1992)
Shared perceptions of the way things are around here.	Climate and culture	Reichers & Schneider (1990, p. 22)
Psychologically meaningful molar [environmental] descriptions that people can agree characterize a system's practices and procedures.	Organizational climates	Schneider (1975, p. 474)

The conceptualization of organizational-climate theory was first introduced by Kurt Lewin (Lewin, Lippitt, & White, 1939) in a psychological climate study titled "Patterns of Aggressive Behavior in Experimentally Created Social Climates." Then it was defined by psychologists George Litwin and Richard Stringer (1968) as described at the beginning of this section. And recently, the late Harvard psychologist David McClelland suggested that organizational climate refers to six key factors that influence an organization's work environment: flexibility, responsibility, standards, rewards, clarity, and commitment (Goleman, 2001), which are defined in Table 2-2.

Table 2-2. Six Key Factors of Organizational Climate

1. *Flexibility*: How free employees feel to innovate unencumbered by red tape.
2. *Responsibility*: Employees' sense of responsibility to the organization.

Continued

3. *Standards:* The level of standards that people set.
4. *Rewards:* The sense of accuracy about performance feedback and aptness of rewards.
5. *Clarity:* The clarity that people have about mission and values.
6. *Commitment:* The level of commitment to a common purpose.

It is important to differentiate between the concept of organizational *culture* and the concept of organizational *climate.* Organizational *climate* refers to the perceptions of organizational practices and procedures that are shared among its members (Schneider, 1975). In contrast, *organizational culture* is a collective experience that emerges from the members' organizational beliefs and social interactions (Schneider et al., 1996; Trice & Beyer, 1993). Culture is based on the underlying values and assumptions and includes those values, beliefs, myths, traditions, and norms among its components. Both climate and culture are real, but they are difficult for people to articulate and almost impossible for leaders to measure.

Although there are some synergies between organizational climate and organizational culture, Table 2-3 illustrates the distinction. For simple differentiation, "organizational climate is a snapshot of the surface features of the culture resulting from a workforce's attitudes and perceptions at a given point and time" (Momeni, 2009, p. 36).

Table 2-3. Differentiation between
Organizational Climate and Organizational Culture

Organizational Climate	Organizational Culture
Flexibility: How free employees feel to innovate unencumbered by red tape.	*Shared values:* A deep sense of purpose that people find meaningful.
Responsibility: Employees' sense of responsibility to the organization.	*Mutual understandings:* Expected behaviors, codes of conduct, dress codes, and so on.

Continued

Organizational Climate	Organizational Culture
Standards: The level of standards that people set.	*Patterns of beliefs*: Unspoken expectations, practices, or decision-making processes.
Rewards: The sense of accuracy about performance feedback and aptness of rewards.	*Expectations of behavior*. Practices that articulate and accomplish what is perceived as right or wrong or good or bad.
Clarity. The clarity that people have about mission and values.	
Commitment. The level of commitment to a common purpose.	

Some experts equate the two terms, but their similarity is better thought of as an overlap and the product of some of the assumptions underlying each concept. Organizational climate is a manifestation of the culture—the tip of the iceberg above the waterline (Fleming, 2001).

Both its climate and its culture have a strong impact on the organization, especially during times of change. The members of an organization describe organizational factors (i.e., the climate) in the same way but interpret them differently because of the cultural influences of an organization (Rosen, Greenhalgh, & Anderson, 1981). For example, authoritative leadership and limited participation in decision making may be viewed as negative by one employee and as positive by another. Therefore, it is important for the leaders of a company to assess the organization's climate and culture simultaneously. This approach enables them to accurately assess the impact of the organization on such measurable aspects as employee satisfaction.

Jeffrey Cernohous stated, "The way that leaders champion core values is by showing their people that they really believe and act under those core values. They are not just sitting up there at a quarterly meeting saying these are their values; it has to happen every day. People know if you're walking the talk" (J. Cernohous, personal communication, July 25, 2014).

This approach to organizational climate is illustrated in the first column of Table 2-4, with possible ways these factors surface above the waterline as the climate within an organization in the second column.

Table 2-4. Six Factors That Surface as Organizational Climate

McClelland Factor	Ways Factors Surface as Climate
Flexibility: How free employees feel to innovate unencumbered by red tape.	• People working together • Decentralization • Self-directed work teams • Freedom and flexibility
Responsibility: Employees' sense of responsibility to the organization.	• People doing quality work • Giving all people access to the financial information and data the organization is using to base its decisions on • Shared responsibility
Standards: The level of standards that people set.	• Listening more than talking • Formal open-door policy • Providing people with the technology and resources they need • Constant learning • Eliminate fear of failure • Reduced status distinctions
Rewards: The sense of accuracy about performance feedback and aptness of rewards.	• Low turnover • Pay tied to company performance • Recognition programs • Formal performance appraisal process • Mentorship program • On-the-job coaching
Clarity: The clarity that people have about mission and values.	• People viewed as a long-term investment • Open architecture • Bulletins and monographs of key issues and company decisions
Commitment: The level of commitment to a common purpose.	• People work until the job is done • Happy employees • Training, workshops, educational opportunities, and assistance

In terms of relationships among employees, Reichers and Schneider (1990) explained that organizational climate is focused on employees' shared perceptions of "the ways things are around here" (p. 22), which then become acceptable norms and expectations that guide their behavior in a particular setting (Schneider, 1983). The employees' perceptions of and attitudes toward their organization at any given time (Momeni, 2009) are of critical importance. At one such people-process culture organization, visitors frequently notice that people working in this environment smile more.

Essentially, climate is a label used to describe the perceptions, temporary attitudes, and feelings of the individuals in an organization (Schneider, 1996). Understanding organizational climate and how to manage it is important, because, today, it is not enough for companies to make a profit. We also expect them (leaders and companies) to do so by doing the right things (outlined in this book) while providing a good workplace environment for their employees.

Traditional relationships between supervisors and employees have evolved over the past few decades from a transactional relationship into a warmer relationship with increased connectedness. Organizations appreciate that these supervisor–employee interactions are not only the right thing to do but also are a key to their success (Levering & Erb, 2011).

The Effects of Organizational Climate on the Organization's Performance

Organizational climate can explain the behavior of people in the workplace. Kaczka and Kirk (1968) found that it affected workplace performance. In their study, an employee-centered climate was associated with higher performance—lower unit cost and higher profits.

In fact, the relationship between climate and employee well-being (e.g., satisfaction and stress) has been widely studied. Because climate is a measure of the major organizational characteristics that workers experience, virtually any study of employee perception of their workplace can be understood as a climate study. These studies link climate factors—leadership, communication openness, participative management, and conflict resolution—with employee satisfaction and, inversely, with dissatisfaction and stress levels (Schneider, 1985). *Stressful organizational climates* are characterized by limited employee participation in decision making, the use of punishment and negative feedback as motivation, conflict avoidance, confrontation in place of problem solving, and negative relationships between the group and its leaders. *Socially supportive climates* benefit employee mental health, leading to lower rates of anxiety and depression (Repetti, 1987), fewer sick days and workers' compensation cases, and less turnover.

Research shows that shared perceptions of undesirable organizational features are connected to low morale and instances of psychogenic illness (Colligan, Pennebaker, & Murphy, 1982). Therefore, to be a high-performance organization (HPO), it is important that employees who interact with each other share common positive perceptions of the organization, that they align with the culture and climate of the organization, which can also lead to positive deviance in the workplace.

In every organization, there are individuals or groups of employees whose uncommon strategies and behaviors enable them to find better solutions to problems than their peers can, despite their access to the same resources and despite facing similar or more difficult challenges; this outcome is called *positive deviance*. Positive deviant behaviors in the workplace may include innovative behaviors, criticizing incompetent supervisors, and noncompliance with dysfunctional directives (Galperin, 2002).

Kathryn Roberts, president and CEO of Ecumen, spoke about the benefit of empowering others in the workplace in a 2014 interview: "We think if you [want to] honor and empower people, you have to listen. People actually have good ideas, and you need to do something about that. So, you may have heard this from Debbie [Cervenka, former executive vice president of Phillips Plastics Corporation]; we have this . . . internationally acclaimed program for dealing with dementia where we remove all inappropriate antipsychotic meds . . . The US does not physically restrain people with Alzheimer's anymore, but we put them all on chemical restraints. It is just easier when they have bad behavior . . . We had one young nurse up in Two Harbors [who questioned the use of certain medications], and somehow she managed to convince her pharmacist and her doctor to quit prescribing these meds [to patients], and [suggested] how to put other behavioral techniques in place . . . [The patients] actually woke up. They weren't wheelchair slumbers anymore. They could feed themselves. They could recognize family members, and they wanted to listen to music. They were astonishing success stories. It is now implemented in every site we have. We are developing [a] curriculum to train any caregiver on the[se] techniques. We have saved hundreds of thousands of dollars in inappropriate medications. We have trademarked the name, and that all came from one woman's . . . idea" (K. Roberts, personal communication, July 9, 2014).

Often studied along with positive deviance are organizational citizenship behavior and positive organizational scholarship. *Organizational citizenship behavior* is a manifestation of the employee's affective commitment to the organization and is likely to benefit his or her performance across business strategies and organizational cultures (Kehoe & Wright, 2013). Organizational citizenship behavior is further defined as "individual behavior that is discretionary, not directly or explicitly recognized by the formal reward system, and in the aggregate promotes the efficient and effective functioning of the organization" (Organ, 1988, p. 4). Whereas *positive organizational scholarship (POS)* is defined by Cameron et al. (2005) as, "dynamics that lead to developing human strength, producing resilience and restoration, fostering vitality, and cultivating extraordinary individuals, units and organizations."

Whether through positive organizational scholarship or organizational citizenship behavior, employees who are committed to the organization may contribute to it in the absence of rewards and may extend their efforts beyond required task performance (Kehoe & Wright, 2013). Such employees thus demonstrate *affective commitment*—positive affection toward the organization—that results in increased levels of commitment reflected through organizational citizenship behaviors, positive organizational scholarship, and positive deviant behaviors. This affective commitment may stem from the employee's perception of being managed effectively or from high-performance human resources (HR) practices embedded in the organization's culture (Kehoe & Wright, 2013). Implications from the intangible and enduring assets of high-performance HR practices and positive employee relations may be a sustainable competitive advantage at the organization level (Fulmer et al., 2003).

CHAPTER 3

The People-Process Culture Approach to Organizational Climate

To achieve the desired people-oriented organizational climate, senior leaders must first make people a priority. Doing this helps their employees find meaning in their work, to put their best efforts forward. Senior leaders should also set values that align with the people-oriented vision proclaimed by the organization. Although they should be set by the organization, deeply shared people-first core values are implicit to a people-process culture. These are the lifeblood of a people-process culture, but it takes senior leadership, HR, and other support systems to help put these values into action. Without them, the organizational climate suffers.

The decisions of founders and other top leaders in the early stages of the organization's life cycle have a profound impact on its development and lead to the creation of strategies, structures, climates, and culture (Schein, 1992; Schneider, 1987). Leaders of people-process culture organizations make an intentional and values-based decision to foster the twin beliefs that *all people are important* and *people working together achieve more.*

Organizational cultures are not inherently good or bad, right or wrong. The key to success, in terms of profitability, is whether the culture meshes with the industry's culture, whether the culture meshes with the organization's culture, and the competitive environment in which the organization operates. When an organization's culture aligns with the industry culture and the competitive environment, the employees find it easy to implement the company's strategy successfully. Organizations do best in terms of productivity, profitability, and engagement when they focus the success of the business through the support and success of the employees. An organizational culture founded on strong values, practices, and norms helps energize its employees to be effective, efficient, and innovative by encouraging and rewarding these traits.

The strength of any culture depends on the degree to which the leadership norms, values, and practices are shared throughout the organization and how they are regarded. A strong culture generally focuses on leadership and consensus. Weak cultures are generally represented by a lack of agreement on norms and values and are generally represented by incongruent leadership behaviors and practices (Driskill & Brenton, 2011). This disconnect can be detrimental to employee morale and productivity.

Strong Organizational Cultures

An organization's culture is strong and cohesive when it conducts business with a clear set of principles and values. Strong cultures are action oriented, with an attitude of continuous improvement of products and processes, and are generally viewed more positively overall by employees and investors, and their efforts generally result in higher profits. The shared values of the company are broadly known within it, limited in number, treated as important, and ranked in terms of their strategic importance to the business (Schein, 2010). The leadership of these organizations carefully communicates the mission and vision of the company, and managers within the organization also tend to form strong cultures within their departments.

When strong cultures align with a strategy and execution plan that are also aligned, the employees are empowered (Schein, 2010), which leads to more employee engagement, quality work, and overall company success. Long-lived or legacy corporations have a powerful sense of identity and organizational culture that creates a sense of belonging that unifies staff members (Driskill & Brenton, 2011). Emotional commitments and a strong work ethic are created and embodied in an image or brand, a sense of pride in the work, loyalty, and a common identity with the organization (Driskill & Brenton, 2011).

Brad Wucherpfennig, in our 2014 interview, provided insight on how strong cultures align. "We don't distinguish much between what is done by the executives, the leads, the engineers, and the superintendents on the job and the craft people. They obviously play different roles on the job. As far as walking out the core values, I believe that we are all involved in that. That comes from the founder, who started out more or less as a craft guy. He went off to college, came back, and did construction. He did a lot of the work himself. That's sort of the gray-collar part of our philosophy: If you know your professional job specialization but you also have knowledge of and know the craft side and the reason you like that . . . Obviously, the jobs are different. The pay is different. But how we are safe on the job, or how we work together as a team, or how we respect one another, or how we do the job that is set in front of us at the first opportunity, doesn't really change by whether you're the president, whether you're the engineer, whether you're the laborer, or the foreman who is in place at thirty stories in the air. The core values are what make the team" (B. Wucherpfennig, personal communication, August 5, 2014).

Strong cultures are closely aligned with high-performance culture characteristics, which generally include the following attributes: culture-reinforcement tools, people-oriented processes, an organizational design focused on results, and an emphasis on achievement and excellence (Moran, Palmer, & Borstorff, 2007). But strong cultures are also intensely people focused. They share these traits: a deeply shared sense of purpose, unrelenting focus, and a physical work environment with which employees report high satisfaction. These organizations treat their employees with respect, foster autonomy and empowerment, focus on relationships, implement mentor programs, strive for accountability, encourage employee initiative, reward and celebrate accomplishments, and set clear standards of performance expectations for their employees (Driskill & Brenton, 2011).

These organizations' recruitment and retention practices are also centered on a good organizational fit, which results in reduced turnover and allows them to benefit from increased cohesion among the employees, teamwork, and job satisfaction. Jeffrey Cernohous said in a 2014 interview, "One of the first things I recognized after getting to know Phillips and the culture a little bit, was that the whole concept of a people-process culture resonated with me. To see things like that all people are important and that people working together achieve more had a tangible impact on my personal beliefs and growth as a future leader of a company. It was definitely one of those life-changing events for me" (J. Cernohous, personal communication, July 25, 2014).

High-performance cultures invest time and resources to empower their employees to be successful. Their metrics are designed and implemented so that success is measured throughout the year, not just at convenient intervals at the middle or end of the year. These organizations encourage regular collaborative goal-setting practices that foster feedback and continuous improvement. However, let us offer a cautionary note: High-performance cultures that focus solely on results may also foster negative consequences for business units or employees who do not consistently meet performance and productivity goals, no matter how legitimate the reasons may be. As a result, business units can be highly scrutinized, sold, or eliminated (Driskill & Brenton, 2011), and employees can be disciplined or terminated for reasons beyond their control. Therefore, a carefully planned strategy using a balanced approach and leadership style that focuses on people is important.

A characteristic of strong cultures is that they create an environment focused on achieving excellence and on high-quality performance measures and products. Their policies and practices are embedded within the organization to inspire employees to perform at their highest level (Driskill & Brenton, 2011). The caveat is that top leaders and managers must actively listen to employee feedback regarding innovation and product ideas and new approaches to doing business. This cultural exchange empowers the employees and will encourage them to excel.

However, strong cultures with practices that do not fit a company's context can also create problems that may lead intelligent people to behave in destructive ways, which can undermine an organization's ability to survive (Kotter & Heskett, 1992; Schein, 2010). Such disconnects between the leader and the culture can have damaging effects on the organizational culture and climate that can create employee resentment and decreased employee engagement.

Weak Organizational Cultures

Weak organizational cultures arise when there is little agreement among organizational members and similarly incongruent leadership regarding the values, beliefs, and norms of the company. The members within the culture may not have a clear understanding of what matters to them. The leader may not have articulated a clear mission and vision for the organization, or there may be conflict between the leader and the organizational members (Driskill & Brenton, 2011). Employees in such organizations generally do not demonstrate loyalty and cannot identify with this vague picture of the mission, vision, and strategy of the organization. Trust is also difficult to foster in such organizations. These factors result in the culture having little meaning or identity for the organization members, employees, and managers alike. Behaviors such as gossiping, manipulation, favoritism, a lack of communication, and competition among employees are the standard rather than the exception in this sort of culture, all of which harm organizational performance (Kabasakal, Asugman, & Develioglu, 2006).

This reality was described well by Charlie Krueger, owner of Krueger Training and Development and professor emeritus at University of Wisconsin (UW)–Stout, in our interview. "Without high levels of trust, you restrict information flow, because people are guarded. They start adapting their behavior around avoiding. When you lose that information, you lose your ability as a leader to make effective decisions. Also, you need to have the brutal facts. You have to know what's wrong with the organization to fix it and keep it on track. I did qualitative interviews and research, then I ran it by a number of different boards. One of the characteristics that we have on there—one of the thirty-six—is that a good department chair shares both the good news and the bad news. They are very open and transparent. So, again, to me, it all gets down to if you don't have trust, you don't have good information. If you don't have good information, you don't make good decisions. If you don't make good decisions, you lose money. And you lose your people. From the standpoint of people, trust is the thing that holds people together. Trust gives people confidence. Trust helps them feel like they can go ahead and do things and take risks" (C. Krueger, personal communication, July 31, 2014).

Weak cultures tend to be associated with lower performance and exhibit characteristics such as insular thinking, a resistance to change, political internal dynamics and environments, and dysfunctional employment and promotion practices (Kabasakal et al., 2006). Obviously, none of these factors is likely to lead to employee retention or to encourage success.

Organizations with weak cultures tend to be focused internally, with a single-minded approach, rather than searching for best practices and continuous improvement measures in their competitors or through employee acquisition. The organizational leaders believe they have all the answers, and communication is nonexistent or remains top down, from the leadership to the employees, with no bottom-up feedback, with the possible exception of a few trusted advisors (Driskill & Brenton, 2011).

Another characteristic of low-performance cultures is a resistance to change. In the current, fast-paced global environment, strong, effective leadership capable of adapting to the ever-changing marketplace is necessary. In low-performance cultures there is a lack of leadership, direction, and encouragement (Driskill & Brenton, 2011), and new ideas are suppressed, because of a desire to maintain the status quo, or become lost in the bureaucratic hierarchy of the organization. The political dynamics involved in such a situation can create risk-avoidance behaviors that can hamper employee initiative, drive, and innovation.

Work environments that are highly political or that involve autocratic styles of leadership tend to be more isolated and resistant to change. The day-to-day operations and issues are vetted through established lines of power and strong coalitions. Such cultures are focused on individual self-interests rather than on the collective interest and shared values of the culture.

Weak cultures are generally inconsistent with promotion and advancement. Individual employees are promoted or advanced into higher positions without an evaluation or consideration of their individual talents and skill sets compared with the primary aspects of the job. This results in an organizational misalignment that negatively affects strategy development and execution, which can be harmful to an organization's long-term health.

Depending on the organizational life cycle of the culture, leaders and managers may become constrained by the culture over time. This may be more evident late in the organization's life cycle, when core beliefs and values are firmly entrenched, which may hamper the company's ability to adapt and innovate (Nieminen, Biermeier-Hanson, & Denison, 2013). The hierarchy and bureaucratic structure become barriers for innovation and productivity. As organizations adapt, products and services change to meet new market realities; leaders and managers need to realize that innovation, technology, and effective leveraging of employee talent create a competitive advantage in the marketplace (Kotter & Heskett, 1992; Schein, 2010).

Weak cultures typically lack cohesiveness, identity, and purpose. Such organizational cultures are generally designed to benefit only a few of their members, usually top organizational executives and CEOs. Such companies lack the organizational glue that a strong embodied culture provides, and their employees become loosely connected to the organization and tend to create their own norms for behavior (Driskill & Brenton, 2011). As a result, when challenges or new opportunities are presented, these companies often find themselves lacking the stamina, drive, and resiliency needed to achieve a competitive advantage. Unfortunately, most organizations will not embark on culture change or realignment until an organizational or economic crisis happens. However, weak cultures can be transformed by visionary leadership, shared values, and sound human-resource and talent-development practices.

CHAPTER 4

High-Performance Organizations

Although the concept of success—of a company's being a high-performance organization (HPO)—is becoming increasingly important among academics, professionals, and managers, the concept is still not well understood. Also, there is no consensus on what it means to be an HPO. In an informal survey, when asked the question, "What is an HPO?" most executives began their response with something related to financial performance. Very few focused on human performance, passion, or purpose as indicators of an HPO.

As this response suggests, it is often assumed that the sole purpose of an HPO is to be profitable. Although this reasoning has been supported with traditional management theory, there is a strong movement to boldly define HPOs as companies that are "fueled by passion and purpose, not cash" (Sisodia, Wolfe, & Sheth, 2014). Looking beyond financial profit, truly successful companies seek personal and society profit as well.

Although there may be a lack of understanding of the HPO concept, there is significant evidence that HPOs drive business results. HPOs that spend the time and money to create and support positive stakeholder relations and cultivate a high-performance work environment are a worthwhile investment that will be repaid with significant returns to the firms. The culture of an HPO shapes its worldview. This, in turn, predisposes behavior in the organization. The hallmark of an HPO is the people-first core values. By creating a people-focused culture with a focus on creating a wonderful environment for employees, the culture sets the tone for employees to also treat customers and other stakeholders well. Ample evidence exists to assert that HPOs that stress humanistic, people-first values produce higher levels of employee productivity, stronger customer loyalty, and higher profit margins.

There are many ways for business leaders, scholars, professionals, and students to characterize an HPO. They could do so on the basis of profitability, return on investment, or corporate social responsibility or could require certain criteria, such as those set forth in the Great Place to Work index (*Latin Trade*, 2010). How one chooses to characterize an HPO is dependent on a number of variables and worldviews. To better grasp the meaning of the term *high-performance organization*, review Table 4-1.

Table 4-1. Characteristics of a High-Performance Organization

Built on love
People-first core values
A happy productive workplace
Welcomed enthusiastically by communities
High levels of trust and open communication among all stakeholder groups
Helps all stakeholders win, including investors
Strong leadership practices that "walk the talk" at all levels within the organization
Helps people find the self-actualization they are seeking
A clearly articulated vision and mission that values people
Responsiveness, adaptability, and a talent for thriving on change
Work environment and human and organizational practices that reflect and align with the organization's core values
Fueled by passion and purpose, not cash
Makes the world better by the way they do business—and the world responds

Here, we define an HPO as an organization that embodies *people-first values*, creates a strong and positive culture of trust among its people, and thus sustains a high level of profitability. HPOs are also referred to as *high-commitment organizations*, *high-involvement organizations*, and *high-performance work organizations*, and the basic premise is to "create an internal environment that supports customer needs and expectations" (Varma, Beatty, Schneir, & Ulrich, 1999).

HPOs are often built on the strong value systems of their founders, but they are always focused on their people. In "Leadership Lessons from Great Places to Work," Mike Murkowski, one of the international vice presidents of marketing at FedEx characterized the role of the company's founder, Fred Smith: Fred "built FedEx on a principle called people–service–profit, which indicates that if we value and invest in our people, they provide superior service to our customers, who then bring us higher profits, which are, in turn, reinvested and shared with our people" (*Latin Trade*, 2010, p. 50).

It is not enough to be the best among mediocre organizations; it takes substantially more to be an HPO. HPOs consistently outperform their competitors and realize bottom-line impacts from their human-capital functions. As part of the talent strategies of an HPO, there is a focus on employee engagement processes, raising performance standards, and identifying and promoting high-potential talent (Hill et al., 2014). HPOs ensure a high-performance environment wherein all stakeholders embrace people-first core values, profit from their human capital, and work together to respond to changing conditions and cultural differences in the economic and global environment.

Organizations that want to become HPOs must establish a collaborative process for articulating and sharing a common vision of what success means to their organization and for aligning stakeholders with these nested visions. These visions are the set of *core values* that drive the company's policies and by which the organization's success is judged.

HPOs have characteristics—people-first core values, passion and purpose as their motivation, and high levels of trust among their stakeholders, to name a few—such as those outlined in Table 4-1. The leadership, business strategies, and HR strategies of the organization are all aligned to create a culture within the organization in which people come first.

Tom Walter, CEO of Tasty Catering, stated in a 2014 interview, "Our people are our most important product. . . . So we leverage our people through [our] core values . . . Our core values support our people. Our people buy into the core values, and the core values buy into the people. . . . I fully believe that employee engagement is the leading indicator of a company's health. . . . The most important key ingredient for employee engagement is leadership. Leaders are always watched. They are watched 24 hours a day. They are listened to, and everything they say that is not exactly correct is repeated rapidly through the company. . . . Their behavior is transparent, whether they like it or not. So we can't have core values if the leaders don't follow them implicitly. So we hold our leaders in our company to an even higher level of the core values. . . . If the culture doesn't match the leader, then it will never work" (T. Walter, personal communication, July 15, 2014).

The following are a few other examples of the characteristics of HPOs that might not be as observable to a customer or client but that have real bottom-line impact:

- decreased turnover;
- decreased workers' compensation claims;
- outperforming competitors and realizing bottom-line impacts from their human capital functions;

- intentional cultural design for bringing out the best in people and thereby producing organizational capability that delivers sustainable business results;
- a sustained organizational environment that leads to the personal development of its employees and profit; and
- the continuous, positive development of people's strengths and character, which, in turn, continuously improves the employees' quality, productivity, and service in these organizations. (Saylor Foundation, 2015).

Just as there is no single consensus definition of an HPO, not all components of an HPO are agreed on either. Table 4-2 illustrates models and the components of HPOs within those models.

Table 4-2. Models and Components of a High-Performance Organization

HPO Scores Model	HPO Framework	Key to Creating Sustainable High Performance	Components of the High-Performing Work Organization
S: Shared information and open communication	Quality of management	Senior leaders' perception of the marketplace	Self-managing work teams and sociotechnical systems
C: Compelling vision	Openness and action orientation	A shared vision, mission, value, and strategies that are aligned with the realities of the marketplace	Employee involvement, participation, and empowerment
O: Ongoing learning	Long-term orientation	Leadership practices that are congruent with the vision, mission, values, and strategies	Total quality management

Continued

HPO Scores Model	HPO Framework	Key to Creating Sustainable High Performance	Components of the High-Performing Work Organization
R: Relentless focus on customer results	Continuous improvement	Infrastructures that support and reinforce the vision, mission, values and strategies	Integrated production technologies
E: Energizing systems and structures	Employee quality	Employee behaviors that meet customer needs	Learning organization
S: Shared power and high involvement			
Source: Blanchard (1999).	Source: The HPO Framework.	Source: Owen, Mundy, Guild, & Guild (2001)	Source: Kirkman, Lowe, & Young (1999)

Academics, professionals, and business professionals are all viable resources who present their own perspectives on the key components of HPOs. Typically, HPOs are designed such that their organizational culture heightens employee performance and the overall effectiveness of the company and produces long-term sustainable positive results.

The five components deemed instrumental to creating and sustaining an HPO are

1. people-first core values,
2. trust,
3. the right leadership and HR practices,
4. meaningful work, and
5. responsible global citizenry.

Regardless of the industry or the company's size, the members at all levels of the organization must agree on the set of core values that drive their organization. They should have a clear understanding of how they want their organization to look, feel, and sound to all stakeholders. Without agreement, the individual members act alone and in isolation, making it untenable for wider stakeholders to arrive at a common understanding of what the organization represents. This makes high performance difficult to achieve.

High Performance Means Profits

To build sustainability, people-process cultures are competitive and results driven. Productivity and profit matter at the individual, team, corporate, and community levels. Making money isn't an option; it's a necessity. These high-performance people-centered organizations are not for the faint of heart. Leaders at many levels need to identify trends quickly and take risks to create new opportunities for people, product development, service, and profit. The following are the primary drivers of the competitive advantage in a people-process culture:

- Profits are the lifeblood of business, and those profits are invested back into the organization's people.
- Open communication increases productivity and profits.
- People are viewed as a long-term investment.
- Happy people yield high returns.
- Profit and people must be viewed over the long term.

The lifeblood of any business is profit. It nourishes company health by providing money for research and development, equipment, and training. With a steady stream of profit, companies can build new facilities, try out new technologies, and launch new ventures. Profits help companies pay their people well, not only in wages but also in an array of flexible benefits, profit sharing, incentive plans, and investments in education and training.

According to Kotter and Heskett (reported in Sullivan, Sullivan, & Buffton, 2002), people-first-value-led companies outperform others: Their revenue grows, on average, four times faster. Their rates of job creation are seven times higher. Their stock price grows twelve times faster, and their profit performance is 750 percent higher.

De Geus (1997) found that organizational longevity does not depend on the ability of a company to return the investment to shareholders; profitability, in the companies he studied, was a symptom of corporate health but not a predictor or determinant of it. In these companies, optimizing capital was secondary to optimizing people. The challenge for leaders is to consider the needs of both the organization and its people—that is, to be practical and humanistic. It's also important that the leader model behaviors in line with the organizational culture and embed them in management systems, such as employee selection, day-to-day supervision, training, and performance evaluation. These latter efforts are what make the core organizational values real (Hultman, 2005). Companies can make a lot of money without following the values and principles of a people-process culture. Downsizing workforces, outsourcing, offshoring, slashing operations, deferring maintenance, and ruthless cost-cutting efforts can elevate stock prices—at least temporarily. Whether these "slash and burn" companies can make double-digit profits consistently and over an extended period of time is questionable.

Happy People Yield High Returns

Increasingly, research is showing that happy people yield high returns. Kotter and Heskett (1992) found that revenues for firms with values affirming the legitimate interests of employees, customers, and stockholders (ownership), and encouraging leadership at all organizational levels (empowerment) increased by an average of 682 percent over an eleven-year period. Employees work harder because of the increased involvement and commitment that comes from having more control over their work; they work smarter, because they are encouraged to build skills and competence; and they work more responsibly, because more responsibility is placed in the hands of employees further down in the organization (Pfeffer & Veiga, 1999). Employees are more productive and satisfied when opportunities exist for them to act like stakeholders (Hultman, 2005).

Organizational culture is an important basis for the work practices of high-performance companies and could be a source of competitive advantage if it is properly nurtured. An HPO reports an apparent course (mission, vision, and strategy), which is embraced by employees at all levels. Teamwork, capability development, and empowerment positively influence organizational performance (Muthuveloo & Teoh, 2013). Schiemann (2007) determined the following factors as primary to effective and equitable employee performance:

- *Alignment*: The extent to which employees are aligned with the strategy of the organization: Is everyone rowing in the same direction?
- *Capabilities*: Talent and the way in which that talent is deployed and how it interacts with information and resources.
- *Engagement*: Going beyond work or job satisfaction, beyond commitment, to a higher level of employee advocacy. At this level, employees serve as ambassadors for the organization.

A positive workplace environment often motivates employees to contribute more positively to the organization. Ogbonna and Harris (2002) concluded that organizational culture leads to organizational performance, and that happens when the culture is widely shared among all employees. Such leadership has a strong link to innovation (Shin & Zhou, 2003), which thereby creates an environment where debate and dialogue are used to make sense of novel ideas and new areas. The ultimate reason for technological innovation is to improve the organization's sustainable performance, and the organization can gain a competitive advantage by introducing new products, which allows the organization to increase market demand (Muthuveloo & Teoh, 2013).

Chancellor Meyer, at UW–Stout, spoke about the importance of organizational alignment, "By aligning operations, one of the things that I will go back to is strategic planning. The beauty of strategic planning is that it can help forge a common vision [or road map] of where you're going. It's like having everything on the big board and everybody can see it. . . . You get lots of points of view. Then [you] try to . . . work on the things that are going to be the most impactful and [the] highest priority for the organization. That's . . . the alignment of operations" (R. Meyer, personal communication, October 6, 2014).

Organizational culture plays an important role in achieving high performance and can be a source of competitive advantage if it is appropriately nurtured, learned, and shared. The challenge for an organization is to create an environment where employees understand and commit to the organization's direction, strategy, and goals.

CHAPTER 5

High-Performance Organizations Are Great Places to Work

In "The Social Dimension of Organizations," author van Marrewijk (2004) documents the distinctive features of truly great workplaces. This attribute was defined by Robert Levering and his team as having

- a strong commitment from the CEO and senior management to being a great place to work by supporting a people-first strategy, manifesting their belief that people are indispensable to the success of the business;
- active communication forums between the employees and management—a truly two-way system of communication, allowing the flow of negative information without fear of retribution;
- the division between management and labor fades away, turning the workplace into a community and creating a perception of a special and unique culture; and
- the employees take pride in their job, their team, and their company.

These employees feel that they can be themselves at work. They celebrate the successes of their peers and their cooperate leadership with others throughout the organization. They take pleasure in their work—and in the people they work with—in a deep and lasting way. They want to stay around for their careers, but also for themselves.

Jeffrey Cernohous shared his definition of success, which requires this close connection between management and the employees: "I would define success with the people-process culture when that organization [is] stressed, people band together rather than scatter. They band together to address it as a team. . . . Your leadership has to live it every day. I think a lot of times it's the little things. It's the engagement [of] everyone in the organization in [the] simple things. When you sit down and have your picnic, it's not like the leaders are over here at one table [and] everybody else [is over there]. And here are the middle managers. You know that you've done okay when there is this intermixing that is almost seamless. When you don't know who runs the line and who owns the business, . . . I think that is something else with the people-process culture: . . . you get to know people. The people get to know each other" (J. Cernohous, personal communication, July 25, 2014).

In a study of the best companies to work for in America, Fulmer, Gerhart, and Scott (2003) "established a link between employee attitudes and organization-level financial performance" (p. 986), which had previously been unstudied. According to the Great Place to Work Institute, "Management unquestionably plays a crucial role in determining what makes any company a great place to work—or a bad one" (*Latin Trade*, 2010, p. 48). Employee engagement and management's support of people-centered policies lead to organizational success.

Great workplaces start with management creating quality relationships. As was found in van Marrewijk (2004), great workplaces are measured by the quality of the following three interconnected relationships:

- the relationship between employees and management,
- the relationship between employees and their jobs or organizations, and
- the relationships between employees and other employees. (p. 8)

Chancellor Meyer, at UW–Stout, said, "I think that strategic planning is a great vehicle to actually allow people to participate, to solicit their ideas. It doesn't mean that everybody's idea is going to be used, but [it's beneficial] to have them engaged even as a group and to have a dialogue to prioritize. . . . It's, first of all, just a great process to be involved with as a leader. To open it up and allow for that participation is very rewarding to the worker and very rewarding to the employee. When you have that level of satisfaction, I think you accomplish a lot more as a team. It's all about team building. . . . Putting the people we serve at the top, . . . I think when you have that sort of structure, you can allow stakeholders to provide their feedback and input for strategic planning. You have a much more robust set of ideas to work with. . . . The people-process culture to me, using strategic planning as a tool, is really about establishing a culture where people are rewarded for contributing to the better whole or the customer that you serve at the top of the pyramid" (R. Meyer, personal communication, October 6, 2014).

Being considered a great place to work offers organizations a multitude of advantages, including better recruiting and stronger community relationships (Romero, 2004). Facts, opinions, and experiences (FOEs), HPOs, and people-process cultures, and those organizations recognized as being great places to work through the Great Place to Work index, AARP's *Best Employers for Workers over 50*, and Working Mother's *Best Companies for Working Moms* embrace a supportive culture in which work and life are balanced (Koppes, 2008). In these organizations, it seems that work–life effectiveness—a mutually beneficial relationship between work and life—is valued as a business imperative and strategic tool for recruiting, motivating, and retaining top talent (Koppes, 2008).

The Great Place to Work Institute's *Trust Index Assessment and Employee Survey* is one starting point for organizations invested in building a better workplace. Great Place to Work analysts precisely measure the underlying level of trust within your organization while making targeted recommendations on how to improve it (http://www.greatplacetowork.net).

Psychologically Healthy Workplaces

According to the APA Center for Organizational Excellence (APA COE, 2015), a *psychologically healthy workplace* fosters employee health and well-being while enhancing organizational performance and productivity. Psychologically healthy work practices can be grouped into the five categories found in Table 5-1.

Table 5-1. Psychologically Healthy Workplaces

Work Practice	Characteristics
Employee involvement	• Self-managed work teams • Employee committees or task forces • Continuous improvement teams • Participative decision making • Employee suggestion forums, such as a suggestion box and monthly meetings
Work–life balance	• Flexible work arrangements, such as flextime and telecommuting • Assistance with childcare • Eldercare benefits • Resources to help employees manage personal financial issues • Availability of benefits for family members and domestic partners • Flexible leave options beyond those required by the Family and Medical Leave Act

Continued

Work Practice	Characteristics
Employee growth and development	• Continuing education courses • Tuition reimbursement • Career development or counseling services • Skills training provided in-house or through outside training centers • Opportunities for promotion and internal career advancement • Coaching, mentoring, and leadership development programs
Health and safety	• Training and safeguards that address workplace safety and security issues • Efforts to help employees develop a healthy lifestyle, such as stress management, weight loss, and smoking cessation programs • Adequate health insurance, including mental health coverage • Health screenings • Access to health/fitness/recreation facilities • Resources to help employees address life problems, e.g., grief counseling, alcohol abuse programs, Employee Assistance Programs (EAPs), and referrals for mental health services
Employee recognition	• Fair monetary compensation • Competitive benefits packages • Acknowledgment of contributions and milestones • Performance-based bonuses and pay increases • Employee awards • Recognition ceremonies

Source: Adapted from *Resources for Employers*, by American Psychological Association (APA), Center for Organizational Excellence, 2015, Washington, DC: APA. Copyright 2015 by APA. Adapted with permission.

HPOs employ the psychologically healthy work practices identified in Table 5-1. They recognize the importance of providing such an environment and commit to establishing programs and policies that enhance the work environment for their employees.

Tom Walter understands the importance of creating a healthy workplace. As he stated in his interview, "[We have strong] organizational resiliency. . . . We follow Fred Luthans on psychological capital. This is deeply ingrained within our company. HERO is the acronym: hope, efficacy, resiliency, and optimism. Our leaders are coached in having hope and self-efficacy [in] reaching goals, the ability to set goals, and psychological resiliency. There isn't a problem that you will ever encounter that someone else hasn't encountered. Those with tough psychological resiliency will overcome that. Then optimism. So then we apply that to the organization. . . . If we have the organizational resiliency, we have the leaders, we have the staff, we have the core values, we have the culture, we have everything we need to succeed. So we approach organization resiliency [that way]. We teach them psychological capital. . . . We won the American Psychological Association's award on March 8, 2014, for the psychologically healthiest small workplace in the United States. I think that it is a direct result of the culture. So . . . that means . . . [we are] creating happy, healthy families" (T. Walter, personal communication, July 15, 2014).

Psychological health is an issue that challenges all organizations, including HPOs, irrespective of the company's size or industry. As a result, the ability for organizations to maximize employee performance is contingent on the organization's leadership capacity and willingness to address issues related to their employees' mental health. The overall effectiveness of an organization is directly affected by how well its leaders manage employee mental health issues. Focus in the past has been on physical health alone, but today, it is clear that conversations must be expanded to also cover psychological health and well-being, including considerations for the individual, the family, and the community.

People-first environments focus on creating quality work environments, which can boost productivity and the bottom line. An organizational culture based on a shared set of values and a deep sense of purpose is meaningful. It serves as a powerful framework and filter for making decisions at all organizational levels. A strong belief in people—employees—shapes a culture, which is crucial for leaders to understand and embrace. The people process is an organizational culture that creates a strong belief in people, which leads to sustained high-level performance and profits over an extended period of time. In people-process cultures, the long-term investment in people is a competitive advantage that fosters and protects the company throughout its life cycle. People-process cultures view risk and failure as a necessary part of growing a business, and organizational learning is the result. Flexible, innovative, adaptive, and focused, these organizations are quick to adapt to changing market dynamics by leveraging the talent of their employees through ideas and brainstorming, and they assist and support employee success through the integration of technology (Cardador & Rupp, 2011).

Leadership That Walks the Talk

Traditionally, leaders are seen as the head of the organization, but more recent literature is now describing the concept of leadership throughout the organization. Inspirational leaders are those in the organization who can inspire the others around them to exceed their personal best. Such leaders are tenacious, committed, and driven by a passion and personal responsibility, not rules and regulations. They are open to new ideas, always pushing the envelope, yet watching and observing. They are people catalysts, coaching and guiding, benevolent yet demanding, and revered for their knowledge. They are problem solvers and constant communicators, fun loving, and friendly.

One of the most important aspects of people-process culture leaders is their authenticity. Through their focus on their employees and stakeholders, they cultivate trust to empower their people with knowledge. Jeffrey Cernohous speaks to the importance of having authentic leadership. "If the leaders don't walk the talk, if you can't interact with people at all different levels, I think without that, you are going to have a hard time. You know it's something that I'm proud of that I was able to learn from Phillips and Bob [Cervenka] . . . I think that when you can create a culture with a high level of integrity and honesty and dialogue and know that people are respected and that you will work through problems together, . . . people start acting and working together to solve the problem cooperatively and collaboratively" (J. Cernohous, personal communication, July 25, 2014).

Chancellor Meyer, at UW–Stout, shared the importance of having leadership that walks the talk. "Our core value systems support the idea of being authentic and honest. It's pretty hard as a leader to sell people on the idea of a people-process culture if you don't walk the talk . . . If the goal is to have all of the employees embrace the values, you better be doing that as a leader. It starts at the top . . . That's why the leader needs to walk the talk. That's one of the first steps in building trust. The organization's success really starts with people understanding their role and how they contribute to it. They need to know that they are going to be empowered to do that. Part of that is developing a trust with them that you are going to support them. Again, it gets back to honesty. If something is not working or somebody is maybe not living up to the core values, then you need to call them on it . . . That's part of trust building. Part of it is being honest and authentic. If you as a leader don't live up to a core value and you make a mistake, . . . you need to admit that. . . . I think that builds trust, too" (R. Meyer, personal communication, October 6, 2014).

Chancellor Meyer, at UW–Stout, spoke further about the importance of authentic leadership. "Walking the [talk is important] . . . Those values aren't just for other areas of the institution or the organization. They are for everybody. It is an important element of being successful as a people-process culture . . . The leaders, and especially myself, [should] model the behaviors [and the values] that are expected of the culture . . . I'm going to try to emulate those, and I am going to try to allow the culture to have feedback on them. I think part of being open and honest about communications is inviting feedback. Sometimes that might not be comfortable. We are not in these jobs [all the time] to be comfortable. We hope that these are enjoyable and enriching experiences, but I think that you have to invite a certain level of discomfort. Typically, if you don't feel a little bit of pain, you might not be growing. Think about the times that you have grown the most in your life. It's probably [because] you were willing to make a change or entertain a change and go through it thoughtfully" (R. Meyer, personal communication, October 6, 2014).

In the area of personal integrity, values pertaining to honesty and fairness are mentioned in every study. Kouzes and Posner (1995) found that honesty was ranked first among the characteristics of admired leaders, followed by being forward looking (setting a vision) and the ability to inspire (motivating people to follow the vision). Unless leaders are honest, nobody cares about their vision.

Successful companies build profits by putting people first, according to management guru Jeffrey Pfeffer (1996). Charlie Krueger shares, "Unless you put people first, you are not going to build the trust and confidence in them that they really make a difference. People need to know that they make a difference and that they are part of the company" (C. Krueger, personal communication, July 31, 2014).

Transparency

Top companies open the books—literally—for all their people, proving transparency and sharing financial and organizational performance information on a regular basis throughout the organization.

Debbie Cervenka discussed how information was shared at Phillips, stating, "all information was shared: If we got a huge opportunity with a great customer, if we lost an opportunity, if we made money, if we didn't make money, if there were efficiency issues or quality issues. All of those things were shared with the people in all of the facilities on multiple levels. We would share it through plant meetings. . . . We posted things on bulletin boards. We had table-top displays in all of the cafeterias. Information was shared with everyone, so that people . . . were equally informed. They were aware of where we had problems [and] . . . where we had opportunities . . . [and] successes" (D. Cervenka, personal communication, July 29, 2014).

People-process cultures practice full transparency—sharing profit and loss data, productivity statistics, cash-flow challenges, stock values, investment strategies, and other financial information with all their people. They want everyone to understand what it takes to run the business and how much it costs. In addition, they equip employees with the information and tools they'll need to cut costs and increase productivity.

Charlie Krueger described the level of shared information at Phillips, "You have to share the information. . . . When Phillips Plastics started out, they shared all of their P&L [profit and loss] statements with employees. They knew what was going on with the business. They knew where the money was going. They knew how much was going into retirements there. [There were a] lot of those people with awfully good retirement packages based on their growth [who were] very open with their communication. . . . I look at open communication the same as I do trust. You've got to be transparent. The more you hide stuff, the more people make stuff up. The more people make stuff up, the worse it gets. Again, it's giving both the good and [the] bad news . . . So I am a big proponent of open communication" (C. Krueger, personal communication, July 31, 2014).

CHAPTER 6

Trust Above All Else

We define *trust* here as the willingness to be vulnerable to the actions of another (De Dreu, Koole, & Steinel, 2000). Trust is essential to collaboration, building connections, and helping develop healthy relationships in the workplace. Trust affects our perceptions, assumptions, attitudes, behaviors, cooperation, and overall performance in an organization. It is also a key component in the organizational success of HPOs.

Leslie Lagerstrom shared how important it is to establish a bond of trust with your employees, "Working with Debbie [Cervenka], she often said, 'You will never get in trouble. I might not agree, and we can talk about it later. . . .' At Phillips . . . risk taking is encouraged. . . . Other employees who came to Phillips beaten down from previous employers had a hard time adjusting to our culture. They often acted tentatively (delaying decisions for fear of getting it wrong) in risk taking for fear of getting in trouble" (L. Lagerstrom, personal communication, June 26, 2014).

Trust is the product of relationships and connections between individuals, between top management and entry-level employees, between organizations and stakeholders, and between organizations and government. A culture of trust in an organization begins with trust among its top leadership, which facilitates strategy implementation. If the leadership team members trust each other, they can more easily build trust with their employees and gather the necessary buy-in to move the organization in the right direction (Bazerman, Curhan, Moore, & Valley, 2000).

Debbie Cervenka spoke in our interview about the importance of trust, "I don't know how companies survive that don't trust their people and [in which the] people can't trust the leadership. If people don't know what's going on, they are going to make it up. That's been my experience. So you might as well tell them what is going on. We have weathered some really tough times. We weathered 2008; it was a really tough time on the company . . . But we trusted our people with that information, as opposed to keeping it at an executive level and having people guess and wonder [why] salaries . . . froze and [why] there [was] not going to be a bonus and all of those things. So it went right back to trusting that . . . the majority of your people . . . were going to use that information to positively help the company . . . We had almost $90 million of automotive business go away overnight with the Chrysler and GM situation. Now, I don't care how well you're run, . . . you can't have that much business go off the books overnight and not have an impact. So when you are near $300 million in sales, it has an impact. But we trusted our people. We trusted sharing information with them. We trusted enabling them to be part of the solution" (D. Cervenka, personal communication, July 29, 2014).

Trust—or the lack of trust—affects how people work together. If there is no trust, everything is much harder to accomplish. Trust is the glue that bonds people together, and it helps improve team and organizational performance. For leaders of an HPO, the key question is whether they are willing to build trust in their organization by being transparent and truthful. Creating a truthful environment builds trust and drives the kind of behaviors, attitudes, and approaches needed for high performance.

Tom Walter spoke of the importance of open communication in building trust. "In a company, there is so much gossip resulting from the lack of transparency—financial transparency, organizational transparency. So much negative energy, so much discretionary thinking is wasted, lost, and tainted by the lack of effective open communication. We do financial transparency . . . Every Wednesday at [a prescribed time], everybody in this organization knows exactly where the profit is that day. . . . Because the inventories are done; everything is done. So we know [whether] we [are] hitting our plan for profitability or not. . . . Everybody knows what they need to do to [get] a raise . . . or . . . a bonus. Everybody understands that. The second one, the hidden one, is the internal communication. . . . Open communication removes that negativity, that negative energy, and turns it into positive energy. . . . It fosters open communication through internal communication and financial transparency" (T. Walter, personal communication, July 15, 2014).

When conditions are threatening, telling the truth is especially needed. In HPOs, "not telling the truth to each other is an act of betrayal" to the stakeholders (Block, 1993, p. 30). When resources are scarce, a workplace environment can become competitive and protective. The leaders of HPOs know that genuine partnership among stakeholders—employees and vendors or suppliers—means telling people immediately about reorganizations, cutbacks, and the cancellation of projects. There may be grieving after a grim announcement or bouts of anxiety that result in lost production, but the loss does not compare to the cost of deceiving the stakeholders or withholding that information (Block, 1993).

Brad Wucherpfennig believes trust is a vital component of the people-process culture. "If you don't have the trust, it's pretty hard to improve productivity and find good processes and systems to be innovative . . . To have a high level of trust, you have to understand what the plan is and how the plan is being implemented and what the various functions and positions are within implementing the plan.

If you don't understand the entire complexity of the business, it can erode the level of trust" (B. Wucherpfennig, personal communication, August 5, 2014).

For many leaders, it's hard to let go and trust employees to make meaningful decisions (Bakke, 2013), but trusting and empowering them through truthful transparency is a necessary step in building a good workplace environment. And those leaders must build that trust from the beginning.

Chancellor Meyer, at UW–Stout, spoke about the difficulty of establishing a sense of trust in an HPO. "When you move into a culture that may have not been as people-process oriented in the past, it takes even more energy and investment from the top to start building that culture. It takes time. If you have been in a culture and there has been mistrust and it hasn't been people oriented, there is going to be a big challenge in building that trust. Trust isn't built quickly. It takes time . . . When things come along that put a ripple in that trust, you have to put a lot more energy into rebuilding that, and it will take time. Authenticity is very important. The word *integrity* comes into play then. Making sure that you follow through on the things that you promise is important as a leader" (R. Meyer, personal communication, October 6, 2014).

Redistributing power by empowering work teams makes the employees feel less vulnerable, but it requires trust to be effective, and the employees, in turn, become more honest (Block, 1993; Robbins, 2013). Best-selling author Robert Levering defined a "great workplace as a place where employees trust the people they work for, have pride in what they do, and enjoy the people they work with" (van Marrewijk, 2004). Furthermore, it is a workplace where leaders, employees, and organizations are constantly learning and bettering themselves.

Teamwork and Decentralization

The people-process emphasis on decentralization and self-managed work groups allows employees opportunities to try to test new ideas and techniques. With teamwork, what one person does is determined by what all others are doing, and the parties must be constantly alert to the ways others are behaving in order to be able to respond appropriately (Jones & George, 1998). This increased sense of responsibility stimulates more initiative and effort on the part of everyone involved. In addition, and perhaps most important, by substituting peers for hierarchical control, a team structure removes layers of hierarchy and absorbs administrative tasks previously performed by specialists, avoiding the enormous costs of people whose sole job it is to watch people who watch other people do the work. Teams also permit employees to pool their ideas to come up with better and more creative solutions to problems (Pfeffer & Veiga, 1999). Organizations designed to support teamwork and decision making at the grassroots level consistently outperform more traditional management structures.

Servant leadership fits within this perspective, because it abstains from a hierarchical approach to employee relations (Lozano, 1998). Instead, it builds on the equality of human beings, stressing coordination through values and individual judgment instead of imposing restrictive norms and enforcement tactics. By giving employees more responsibilities, this form of organization has the potential to utilize the full talents and competencies of employees (Schoemaker, Nijhof, & Jonker, 2006). Whether change is invigorating or devastating hinges on the quality of leadership provided at all levels in the organization. The signs of outstanding leadership appear primarily among the people being led in terms of their personal leadership, self-confidence, and engagement in the organization.

People work harder because of the increased involvement and commitment that comes from having more control and say in their work; people work smarter because they are encouraged to build skills and competence; and people work more responsibly because of more responsibility. Along with other factors such as size and industry—even when profits were statistically controlled in the research—the value the organization placed on HR, such as whether the company cited employees as a source of competitive advantage and how the organization rewarded people, was significantly correlated with the probability of the organization's survival (Pfeffer & Veiga, 1999). Increased responsibility can also lead to passion and pride for organizations. A family-like environment emerges in which employees work in a harmonious manner (Duxbury & Gover, 2011). A family environment often exists in small organizations, but as the size of the family grows, there is a tendency for factions or silos to emerge (Weymes, 2005). A family environment cannot be engineered, because it is the result of the interactions between the individuals and the core values of the organization.

At Baker Concrete and Construction, lending a helping hand to fellow employees is par for the course. Brad Wucherpfennig revealed, "We have a lot of respect for the craft people doing the work. Our coworkers may themselves take care of one another. When a coworker is in a remote location in the field for an extended period of time, their family may have needs while they are away. We have coworkers who help the families of other coworkers. We have a charitable fund for projects that cause financial hardship. There have been a lot of different things that we have done including tuition assistance for their children" (B. Wucherpfennig, personal communication, August 5, 2014).

Chancellor Meyer, at UW–Stout, spoke to the importance of collaboration as a critical element in the people-process culture.

"Collaborating is big. It's where our students are going. They need to be able to collaborate . . . I think respect as an operating style or tenet is extremely important. The people-process culture is built on respect. Within that environment, you can disagree, but you can do so respectfully, and you can learn from each other's positions. Supporting diversity and inclusion is important. We state that right on our Web page. It's something that we really believe in . . . Diversity to me means even more than even race and gender. It means diversity in thinking, too, and respecting that not everybody is going to agree with you or they will have different ideas. That makes . . . a very rich environment" (R. Meyer, personal communication, October 6, 2014).

One of the greatest payoffs is that teams substitute peer-based control for hierarchical control of work. Team-based organizations also are largely successful in having all the people in the firm feel accountable and responsible for the operation and success of the enterprise, not just a few people in senior management positions. This increased sense of responsibility stimulates more initiative effort from everyone involved (Sagiv et al., 2011).

High Levels of Trust

In an age characterized by cynicism, doubt, and limited trust within organizations, leaders who passionately believe in and practice respect for their people are discovering that they have a powerful new business ally: trust. Fostered by open communication and making good on corporate promises, trust is emerging as one of the single most important ingredients in helping people and organizations perform at their highest level and beyond. People who trust each other work together more efficiently. Trust enhances listening and communication skills by reducing emotional barriers (Osborne & Cowen, 2002).

Armed with clear goals and free from worry about hidden agendas, employees can focus on getting the job done.

People are disposed toward fairness, a necessary condition for trust and trustworthiness. This tendency toward trust and reciprocity is balanced by a willingness to punish those who fail to act fairly, even at a cost to themselves. Cultural variations are very likely and condition the degree to which people are willing to trust others (Fichman, 2003). With unconditional trust—in which shared values create a common bond—a different scenario occurs: People begin to feel that they are not merely coworkers or business acquaintances but colleagues, friends, or team members. In other words, although the presence of conditional trust allows a group to work toward a common goal, the existence of unconditional trust can fundamentally change the quality of the relationship and can convert a group into a team.

Conversely, when they lack aligned core values or investment in the relationship, people are less likely to cooperate. There is no assurance of shared values that would orient the parties to the future, and their relationships are less likely to be positive (Jones & George, 1998). If individuals do not trust and respect each other, passion may not exist throughout the organization, and employees may feel some pride for their employer, but the organization will not be a family. The working environment is unlikely to be harmonious.

Unconditional trust also promotes seven kinds of social processes that can lead to the development of synergistic team relationships in an organizational setting. In turn, these can lead to superior performance. These organizational structures incorporate

1. broad role definitions,
2. communal relationships,
3. high levels of confidence in others,

4. help-seeking behavior,

5. the free exchange of knowledge and information,

6. a subjugation of personal needs and ego for the greater common good, and

7. high levels of involvement (Jones & George, 1998).

These social processes are depicted in Figure 6-1.

Figure 6-1. Proposed Effects of Unconditional Trust on Interpersonal Cooperation and Teamwork.

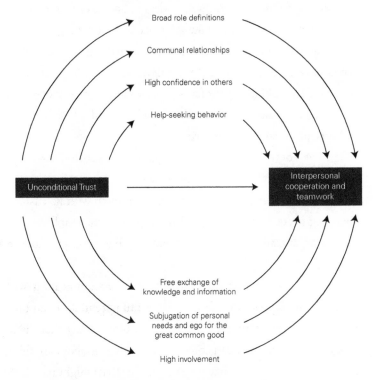

Today, the chief executive is challenged with the task of building trust and integrity in the organization. When trust pervades the organization, there is commitment from the staff and support from the external community (Weymes, 2005). High levels of trust lessen people's resistance to change and help reduce the fear of failure, a critical ingredient in encouraging risk taking. Kathryn Roberts described this fear of risk taking and how she addresses it by walking the talk herself: "Here is one more thing about being a people-process culture. If you empower, honor, and innovate, it means that some things are going to work and some things are not going to work. So, we talk all the time about 'failing forward.' We leaders . . . go out of [our] way to [encourage new ideas], ... I take a chance every time I get in front of [my] employees. I say, 'I am going to try something different today. It's going to be a grand experience. It might be a total flop, and I will be able to tell by looking at your faces or we will have great success, but thanks for coming along for the ride.' I try and model that behavior" (K. Roberts, personal communication, July 9, 2014).

High levels of trust between the company and its customers, forged by follow-through and healthy doses of two-way communication, fosters innovation by keeping the organization in touch with its customers' changing needs and challenges. This empowers the employees and enables the organization to spot new trends and business opportunities more quickly.

Jeffrey Cernohous tied the topic of open communication with empowering employees to perform to their full potential, "I can honestly say that everyone in my organization [knows that] there is an open-door policy, that they can come in and talk to me about anything. Often, . . . it is about things that are going on or [that] might have been a [mistake]. Or [they] might give me a heads up that there is a customer [who] is upset about [something]. The fact that they keep coming tells me . . . we are doing something right. Where I get concerned is if I am finding out about things, and I'm surprised constantly. Because that tells me . . . people are concerned about the ramifications. . . . It's intertwined with trust and communication. They will know [that] if there is a problem, . . . I will be the first one to engage and help if they need the help or empower [them] and say . . . you can deal with this. . . . The whole people process starts with people, having the right people. . . . [It is] a system and a process that empowers people to do the job in the best way that they can and [to] make decisions. Again, I think if you were to ask the team here, it's not an organization that passes blame. It's really about solving problems together as a team. I think that is . . . [an] effective way . . . tied directly to [the] empowerment of people" (J. Cernohous, personal communication, July 25, 2014).

Empowerment is only likely to enhance cooperation and, ultimately, organizational performance, however, if trust exists in an organization. In order to promote trust between two or more parties, managers must understand how an individual experiences trust in others and how trust evolves between people over time (Jones & George, 1998). In order for organizations to have real synergy among their members, those members must develop unconditional trust. This is because only unconditional trust promotes intense interpersonal cooperation and synergistic relationships (Jones & George, 1998). Organizations that choose to encourage the development of unconditional trust among their employees benefit, especially in terms of cooperation and teamwork that promote high performance and competitive advantage (Jones & George, 1998).

Work performed under more oversight and control may always be perceived as better than the identical work performed with less oversight in terms of traditional management models. The effect will be a particularly strong belief for the person doing the supervision. In real work settings, these social psychological processes are counterbalanced by pressures to achieve results and less by the knowledge that participation and empowerment may be helpful in improving performance (Pfeffer & Veiga, 1999). Little evidence exists that being an aggressive or micromanaging boss is necessarily associated with business success. The financial results from these bosses' companies vary from superb to pathetic.

People-process cultures trust their people and view them as a competitive advantage. Brad Wucherpfennig stated, "It's the attitude that you bring to the meeting and to the workforce with the outside world, as well as the attitude you bring to the inside world and the meetings there. I think empowering the people to make decisions quickly on the jobsite allows us to deal with quality issues on the jobsite. We listen to all ideas. . . . We like innovation and take it from wherever it may come" (B. Wucherpfennig, personal communication, August 5, 2014).

CHAPTER 7

Communication Is Vital to Success

Open communication becomes the heart of the organization through the members' forging relationships with key constituents; developing trust; and circulating critical data, ideas, challenges, and solutions. Open communication means much more than extolling management's sanitized version of reality in newsletters, slogans, and videos; it means telling the truth and reality of the business by giving all people access to the financial information and data the organization is using for decision making and forecasting.

Work group meetings, customer contacts, training seminars, quarterly plant meetings, shift representatives or liaisons, and other face-to-face sessions all represent key, two-way channels of communication. Managing, learning from, and acting on the knowledge and wisdom generated by this ongoing exchange makes organizational communication a bottom-line business result. The more people know, the better they will perform. Communication keeps employees from reinventing processes and procedures and facilitates organizational learning. To achieve results, open communication requires ongoing systems and processes designed to provide and capture reliable information on a real-time basis. By keeping communication in the open, problems and issues can be identified early and addressed quickly, thereby saving time and money.

Open communication requires strong leadership and a deep level of commitment among all managers, supervisors, and corporate executives. Walking the talk on the production floor, as well as in the corporate handbook, is essential. Leadership is practicing respect for people. Being a good communicator means being a good listener. Good leaders listen first, using active listening skills and a genuine desire to know how things are working. Leaders need to pay close attention to symbolic communication as well. Simple acts—emptying garbage, sweeping off the sidewalk, for example—communicate volumes about respect for people and the tasks they perform. Open communication builds relationships with employees.

Open communication is one of the trademarks of a people-process culture. In our 2014 interview, Jay Kirihara, owner of Farley Sales Group, spoke about the importance of open communication: "Open communication is so important. . . . Here is this thing we call the hierarchy of communication, and it is harder today because you have texting . . . and emails, but I always tell my team that you . . . have to respond in an equal or higher interactive method when anyone tries to communicate with you. So if somebody calls you and you email them back, that is not acceptable. You either call them back or you meet with them. The reason . . . is [that] if someone calls you, it is kind of important. Or if someone comes to your door, it's important. [You want to honor their needs and respond accordingly]" (J. Kirihara, personal communication, July 23, 2014).

The Impact of Traditions, Rituals, Legends, and Ceremonies

Traditions, rituals, legends, and ceremonies strengthen and sustain organizational culture. Schein (2010) defined culture as "a pattern of shared basic assumptions that the organization learned as it solved its problems of external adoption and internal integration, to be taught to new members as the correct way to perceive, think, and feel in relation to those problems" (p. 18). Ceremonies are important for the communication of a culture's symbols, and they assist in developing an understanding of the culture, integrating new members, and defining what is appreciated and rewarded (Trice & Beyer, 1993). Ceremonies are often structured within the stories, myths, and legends that are told by employees within an organization. These ceremonies also potentially shape and motivate the workforce: The listeners are inspired to do similar things, to continue the story, and to be part of the legend. Stories act as vehicles to communicate lessons and priorities within the culture. This facilitates employees' ability to internalize the cultural artifacts, the espoused beliefs and values, and the underlying assumptions of the organization.

Internalization and identification informs employees as to who they are within an organization, based on their collective thoughts, feelings, and behaviors (Armenakis, Brown, & Mehta, 2011). The espoused beliefs and values are consciously developed as formal organizational practices, such as strategies, goals, policies, and procedures, and as informal practices, including shared histories, traditions, rituals, and legends that become implicit norms of the culture, defining the organizational values and becoming an important role in strengthening and sustaining organizational culture (Schein, 2010). The leadership uses shared value statements, and positive symbols and other forms of nonverbal communication are critically important in building and sustaining a robust corporate culture. Strong, high-performance cultures leverage tradition, rituals, ceremonies, and stories to bring to life these attributes of culture and organizational possibilities and to further strengthen and sustain the organizational culture.

Organizational values commonly include innovation, attention to detail, an orientation toward outcomes or results, and an emphasis on growth, among any number of possible values. Less obviously positive values, such as aggressiveness within the company and with its market competitors may also be important to the organization's internal culture. A careful assessment of what traditions, rituals, and ceremonies are performed within the company can help you determine the organizational culture, but these tools can also be used to deliberately shape it: Symbols and language specific to the organization convey meanings and values that the employees bond with (Driskill & Brenton, 2011). Choosing the stories—creating the legends—that are told in the company and the rituals and ceremonies performed by its members can guide the culture toward a desired set of values.

Sharing the Dream

Employees should be involved in the design of the systems and processes to provide them with the information required to fulfill their role in the organization. This value system extends beyond the employees to include all organizational stakeholders: customers, suppliers, owners, and community members. Through sharing the dream and the storytelling of legends, an organization creates a pride of association with individuals inside and outside the organization. The organization must first share its dream internally, to gain the commitment of the staff to the organization's purpose. Within the company, everyone is important, everyone is a member of the team, and everyone is expected to contribute. Most important, all employees are asked to put the golden rule (treat others as you would like to be treated) into practice on a daily basis.

The dream of success and what that means must also be shared externally—with customers, suppliers, distributors, shareholders, and other members of the community. Externally, the dream is captured in the brand of the organization. Customers are proud of being associated with the brand, communities are proud to have the organization located in their backyard, and suppliers are proud to be associated with the organization (Weymes, 2005). Although an organization requires customer loyalty, it cannot focus solely on the customers; it also needs to manage its relationships with other stakeholder groups (Weymes, 2005).

People-process culture leaders hold all people and systems in the organization accountable to the values, beliefs, and practices embedded in a high-performance corporate culture. They practice open communication and open-door management. Decisions aren't made in a vacuum, with executives huddled in secrecy behind closed doors, but out in the open involving all employees. Financial information is shared with everyone, creating optimal levels of transparency.

Debbie Cervenka stated, "We leveraged people and our values by being an open book, by sharing information, by sharing successes, by sharing things that didn't go so [well]. . . . Our people were informed, and because our people were informed, they felt . . . they were part of the solution. So that became critical, especially as we grew. . . . So it was that process of letting people be a part of that answer" (D. Cervenka, personal communication, July 29, 2014).

Leaders of people-process culture organizations value diverse opinions. In a global marketplace, such leaders expect employees to ask questions, challenge assumptions, and seek new options. Employees and transformational leaders know that intelligent disagreements lead to better decisions and unique solutions (Shin & Zhou, 2003). A shared vision and shared values drive change in people-process cultures. Focused on nurturing people and know-how, these cultures are uniquely positioned to thrive in today's knowledge-based economy.

Communities of Practice

Communities of practice are the informal social networks that support professionals to develop shared meaning and to engage in knowledge building among the members (Hara, as cited in Hara & Schwen, 2006, p. 95). Communities of practice have been long established in the occupational sector. Housed in business-unit sectors, these centers can offer a wide variety of business- and industry-related subjects. People-process cultures, by their inherent design, foster and support communities of practice because the culture's focus is on the greatest assets in the organization—the employees. Hara and Schwen (2006) identified communities of practice as comprising five elements:

1. the development of a shared meaning,
2. informal social networks,
3. a supportive culture,
4. engagement in knowledge building, and
5. individual negotiation and development of professional identities.

Development of a Shared Meaning
Developing a shared meaning requires information to be exchanged and communicated among the members of the organization. Shared meaning may occur through explicit knowledge, often in terms of

industry-related courses or basic academic areas, such as math, reading, language arts, writing, science, and social studies.

Informal Social Networks

In informal social networks, the participants assist each other in informal learning strategies and practices. They share common experiences and give contextual meaning to topics that assist in knowledge transfer and retention.

Supportive Culture

Communities of practice develop a supportive culture in which their members exhibit high levels of trust and camaraderie for each other. Information is shared to support the others' work, and feedback is given to assist the members in learning and development.

Engagement in Knowledge Building

Communities of practice engage in knowledge building through personalized learning. Their members become autonomous learners who take responsibility for their learning. (Hara & Schwen, 2006, pp. 97–98).

Individual Negotiation and Development of Professional Identities

The members of communities of practice learn from each other, developing knowledge and expertise through learning. The communities of practice influence each other to allow their members to become better professionals in their field and to build professional identities or expertise (Hara & Schwen, 2006, p. 107).

Communication as Strategic Thinking and Planning

Staying on the leading edge of change requires top-level communication and access to information to shape day-to-day business operations. As a result, progressive companies are becoming more transparent, opening the books to employees to involve and engage them more fully in the business. Companies that practice open communications management do the following:

- Employees receive ongoing training and education about how the company operates, invests, and makes money.
- Employees have complete real-time access to operational and financial data, including profit and loss statements.
- Employees have a stake in company results and outcomes via profit sharing, employee stock and ownership plans, and other mechanisms.
- Employees share responsibility for keeping track of and influencing business outcomes and results.
- Employees are encouraged to identify and take advantage of new business opportunities.
- Supervisors, team leaders, and corporate executives practice an open-door policy and encourage all employees to use it.
- Multiple communication channels (e.g., traditional, electronic, social media) are used for sharing information throughout the company.
- Internal communication (both formal and informal) is given the same—or greater—priority and quality as external communication and marketing.
- Problem solving and decision making are conducted in the open, and opinions and ideas are solicited openly.

- Company leaders walk the talk in how they communicate, behave, and relate to employees and all other key constituents.
- People have a high degree of trust for management and for each other.

Even building architecture is a form of communication. People-process cultures facilitate creativity and communication through architectural design. Open architecture can facilitate collaboration: Open walls, open doors, and open spaces encourage people to share ideas, challenges, and time with each other. The "all people are important" truth is shown not only in the company's flat organizational structure, but also in building design, natural lighting, and environmentally sustainable buildings and grounds. Architecture can be a powerful transformative agent. People-process cultures use architecture and facility design to communicate core values.

Debbie Cervenka commented on the importance architecture can have on transparency and aligning operations with work environments. "Early on, our plants were very primitive. That was all the company could afford. They were metal buildings with small little offices and very few windows. When we built our fastener plant in Chippewa, . . . it was the first time that we employed an architect. Bob felt that if people on the floor could see what people in the offices were doing and people in the offices could see what people on the floor were doing that we would dispel a lot of [myths]. So we started building facilities with the same openness and communication. The same openness and information sharing now became an open plant design. We had beautiful facilities. We had customers coming in that would say that [we] spent too much money on architecture, [that they] . . . really like[d] that old plant up in Phillips. We would try to say, but we can show that profitwise the more that people know what is going on, [the more they will] take pride . . . in what they are doing. We could prove it profitability-wise—that architecture [is part of] walking the talk" (D. Cervenka, personal communication, July 29, 2014).

Knowledge transfer requires that an individual or a group cooperate with others to share knowledge and achieve mutual benefits (Martins & Meyer, 2012). Martins and Meyer (2012) further emphasized the importance of communication among staff members. People-process cultures place a premium on open communication, using tools such as information systems. *Information systems* are arrangements of people, data, and processes that interact to support daily operations, problem solving, and decision making in organizations (Martins & Meyer, 2012). Recognizing that informed, involved, and knowledgeable workers are more productive and insightful, people-process cultures use a variety of techniques, from information systems to visual cues and face-to-face meetings (Martins & Meyer, 2012).

In today's global marketplace, creating a competitive advantage hinges on how people communicate with each other, relate to one another, and work together. Strategic management and effective communication can improve teamwork, build trust, and enhance creativity. By building positive relationships among team members, effective communication can also shorten production cycles, accelerate decision making, and reduce waste. Ineffective, incomplete, or inconsistent information at any step during this process can derail production schedules and hurt quality, causing unhappy customers to send their business elsewhere.

The following statements describe success and sustainability in a people-process culture:

- Communication is vital to success.
- Open doors and transparency build trust.

- Listening is more important than talking.
- Communication is a shared responsibility of all.

Organizational communication is a shared responsibility in a people-process culture. Weaving communication into the fabric of the company means that communication, public relations, and marketing are considered a part of every person's job description. If employees are not equipped with these at the time they are hired, the company needs to provide all team members with ongoing training, coaching, mentoring, and support. Having employees understand each facet of the business allows for focus on solving problems in order to communicate effectively with customers. Working together and sharing information across business units and geographic areas provides a more cohesive message and creates a competitive advantage in the marketplace. Such communication practices increase and encourage commitment, interpersonal relationships, quality of information exchange, feedback, dialogue, and persuasion. This type and quality of communication decreases misunderstanding and conflict and results in increased cooperation, participation, and group cohesion (Kara & Zellmer-Bruhn, 2011).

Today, more than ever, competitive advantage hinges on how people communicate with each other, relate to one another, and work together. As a strategic organizational function, effective communication improves teamwork, builds trust, and enhances creativity. By building positive relationships among team members, effective communication can also shorten production cycles, accelerate decision making, reduce waste, and create sustainable organizations that support both employees and the communities in which they work and live.

CHAPTER 8

Leadership and Organizational Culture

Where do the tenets of an organization begin? Organizations do not form spontaneously; rather, they are created for a specific purpose. The content formation of organizational culture begins with the decisions made by organizational leaders—in other words, the CEO. Creating and managing organizational culture is the single most important role of the leader (Schein, 2010): CEOs and top leaders set the tone of the culture by defining the goals of and for the organization, which are then operationalized throughout the company (Schneider et al., 1996).

For instance, an organization's goal of benevolence—of preserving or enhancing the welfare of their clients or customers through the company's services—or of providing a product that is beneficial as well as profitable is set by the CEO, who must then pass that information down through the organization.

The leaders and HR professionals of an HPO can be thought of as *connectors*. Author Malcolm Gladwell used the term *connector* in his best-selling book *The Tipping Point* to describe individuals who have many ties to different social worlds (Gladwell, 2000). Connectors are significant because of their ability to link people, ideas, and resources (Ibarra & Hansen, 2011). In HPOs, leaders facilitate collaboration between all stakeholders through the connections they create. Furthermore, they can bring people together from different disciplines, backgrounds, generations, and cultures and leverage all those individuals have to offer (Ibarra & Hansen, 2011). These connections allow for the development of creativity, innovation, and problem solving among stakeholders while promoting a healthy workplace environment. It is important that the leaders of HPOs set the tone by not engaging in political games and turf wars but, rather, by being good connectors and collaborators themselves and assigning clear decision rights and responsibilities (Ibarra & Hansen, 2011). Connectors also understand the importance of establishing the appropriate point person to end the discussion when needed and to make a final call (Ibarra & Hansen, 2011).

HPOs that employ connectors as leaders may have a significant competitive advantage because of the shift during the past several decades from viewing employees as necessary for completing the required work to viewing them as assets, then to treating them as human beings capable of accomplishing amazing things. People have been observed accomplishing amazing things in the very best and the very worst environments. However, organizations that have outstanding workplace environments teeming with spirit and energy *and* exceptional talent strategies tend to attract and retain top talent (Hill et al., 2014).

Connectors and leaders of HPOs may increase their competence and change their mental models through a careful analysis of their behavior. These individuals may risk an intensely threatening emotional experience (Mezirow, 2000) when moving through the four essential steps:

1. critical self-reflection on their behavior;
2. identification of values or assumptions underlying the behavior;
3. changes in underlying values or assumptions; and

4. changes in the behavior (La Venture, 2013; Heorhiadi, La Venture, & Conbere, 2014).

Upon moving through these steps after workplace problems occur, leaders may discover that there is a deficiency in their leadership style that needs to be corrected. During critical self-reflection of his behavior, Dennis Bakke stated that he "soon realized that the more decisions I made, the less engaged others became, and the less ownership they had in the results. The problem was me" (Bakke, 2013, p. 201).

The leaders of HPOs understand that they are sometimes part of the problem. In "Leadership Lessons from Great Places to Work" (*Latin Trade*, 2010), even Mike Murkowski, vice president of marketing, customer service, technology, and experience in FedEx's Latin America and Caribbean Division, understood the importance of self-reflection, understanding social cues, and mindfulness of his tone of voice to having positive interactions among his team. In many instances, change in behavior translates to increased productivity and effectiveness in the workplace (La Venture, 2013).

Leaders consciously and unconsciously embed their tendencies and preferences into their organizations through a variety of mechanisms, such as metrics; criteria for the allocation of rewards, such as profit sharing and bonuses; and personnel decisions (Schein, 2004). The most influential of these practices are leadership, recruitment, onboarding, reward-system alignment, decision-making processes, and organizational learning (Schein, 2010; Verbos, Gerard, Forshey, Harding, & Miller, 2007).

Charismatic leaders embed their personal characteristics into their organizations by establishing organizational goals. These goals attract people with similar personality characteristics, which establishes the *organizational fit* of individuals within the organization (Giberson et al., 2009).

Charlie Krueger discussed the importance of organizational fit in a 2014 interview. "You need to make sure that you have the right people on the bus," he said, "and the wrong people off the bus. You need the right people in the right seats, and then you do the team building. Otherwise, you're going to create a monster, and it's going to be hard to deal with" (C. Krueger, personal communication, July 31, 2014).

Leadership, culture, and strategy are interrelated. Leaders further reinforce organizational culture through secondary articulation or reinforcement mechanisms, such as organizational design and structure decisions, stories and myths, and formal statements (Schein, 2010). Effective leaders also continually shape the culture through their strategic vision, determining what receives attention and what is celebrated (Hartnell & Walumbwa, 2011). Successful execution of strategy requires a supportive organizational culture. Organizational strategies that make good business sense often fail because the underlying shared values of the culture do not support the new approach and are not adopted by the employees. This failure furthers and enables resistance within the culture (Yahyagil, 2006).

The organizational goals set by the leadership can be used not only as metrics for the cultural fit of an employee but also as motivation tools. For instance, individual achievement can be motivated by acknowledging or rewarding that achievement. An organizational goal of power can be encouraged by giving employees power over their own resources.

Although charismatic CEOs and leaders shape organizational culture, cultural norms and expectations must be disseminated throughout the organization. *Cultural carriers*—the formal and informal leaders throughout the organization—reinforce the thoughts and actions of the cultural leader; this support is known as *walking the talk* (Armenakis et al., 2011). These manifestations are interpreted, evaluated, and enacted in varying ways because cultural members have differing interests, experiences, responsibilities, and values (Martin, 2005). Therefore, what leaders do and how those actions are carried through and manifested in the culture are more of a determinant of effectiveness than what leaders believe or value, because the manner in which beliefs and personal values manifest in the day-to-day actions of leaders can vary widely, depending on a range of task and situational factors (Nieminen et al., 2013). These become the motivational drivers for success within the organization (Clercq, Fontaine, & Anseel, 2008).

Brad Wucherpfennig, president of Baker Concrete and Construction, described such motivational drivers in a 2014 interview: "In my opinion, the greatest challenge to that type of culture is in the harder times. It is easier to walk the talk and have a smile on your face when you're making money and times are good. That's not the world in construction. I think that it has to do with profits for a construction firm. It's the ability to make sure that you at least break even in the downturns, which can be sharp and severe. I would rather give up a point of profit on the upside to make sure that I protect it on the downside. The real rubber meeting the road is when you actually walk that talk in the hard times. I think that's the challenge of the people process" (B. Wucherpfennig, personal communication, August 5, 2014). Table 8-1 provides a list of common organizational goals and definitions that are espoused by leaders within organizations.

Table 8-1. Motivational Values

Goal	Definition
Achievement	Personal success through demonstrating competence according to social standards
Benevolence	Preservation and enhancement of the welfare of people with whom one is in frequent personal contact
Conformity	Restraint of actions, inclinations, and impulses likely to upset or harm others and violate social expectations or norms
Hedonism	Pleasure and sensuous gratification for oneself
Power	Social status and prestige, control, or dominance over people and resources
Security	Safety, harmony, and stability of society, of relationships, and of self
Self-direction	Independent thought and action; choosing, creating, and exploring
Stimulation	Excitement, novelty, and challenge in life
Tradition	Respect, commitment, and acceptance of the customs and ideas that traditional culture or religion provide the self
Universalism	Understanding, appreciation, tolerance, and protection for the welfare of all people and nature

Source: Definitions of motivational types of values in terms of their goals (adapted with permission from "Value Priorities and Subjective Well-Being: Direct Relations and Congruity Effects," by L. Sagiv and S. H. Schwartz, 2000, *European Journal of Social Psychology*, 20, pp. 177–198).

Effective Leadership and Organizational Climate

A *positive organizational climate*—a good workplace environment—is often the by-product of effective leadership. Most senior executives today agree that effective leadership is crucial to superior business performance. They recognize that the effectiveness of an organization's leaders can be the difference between being a good and being a great organization. They also understand the profound impact the decisions of founders and other top leaders in the early stages of the organization's life cycle have on the development of that organization and that those decisions lead to the creation of strategies, structure, climate, and culture (Schein, 1992; Schneider, 1987).

One such example is that of the founder of a people-process culture organization who shepherded the company's growth from a small, rural start-up company in 1964 to an organization that employed 1,600 people and generated annual sales of $300 million prior to being acquired. In an interview, the people-process culture founder stated, "I believe the people process—how people work together, how they treat each other, the values they share—is critical to business success. It's the lifeblood of our organization." This people-first philosophy permeated through every aspect of this organization. Simply put, the decisions of the founders and their leadership practices shape everything from the way the company recruits and rewards employees to the ways they delight customers, incubate new businesses, and support community activities. The leadership philosophy of the founders and the leadership practices in action within an organization shape the attitudes, perceptions, and behaviors of its employees, thus affecting organizational climate.

Moreover, Grojean, Resick, Dickson, and Smith (2004) found in their research that leaders not only directly influenced the behavior of the organization's members, but their actions also influenced the perceptions of those members. Such actions defined the norms and expectations of appropriate conduct ingrained in the organization's climate. In fact, according to Momeni (2009), "more than 70 percent of organizational climate directly results from a manager's morale and behaviors" (p. 46). Furthermore, "because behavior is understood to result from emotions and perceptions, *emotional intelligence* has an important effect on behavior" (Momeni, 2009, p. 46). Emotional intelligence "refers to an ability to recognize the meaning of emotions and their relationships, and to reason and problem-solve on the basis of them. [Emotional intelligence] is central to an individual's capacity to perceive emotions, assimilate emotion-related feelings, understand the information of those emotions, and manage them" (Ciarrochi, Forgas, & Mayer, 2001, p. 9). Emotional intelligence is further defined as one's ability to manage and monitor one's own emotions, to recognize different types of emotions in others, to distinguish the difference between one's emotions and those of others, and to possess the ability to direct information toward one's decision-making actions (Mayer & Salovey, 1993). Emotional intelligence has been identified as a measure for distinguishing superior leadership skills and abilities (Pool & Cotton, 2004, as cited in Pinos, Twigg, Parayitam, & Olson, 2006). The results of Momeni's (2009) study show that a manager's emotional intelligence has a positive association with organizational climate.

According to Momeni (2009), "Researchers believe that the behavior of a manager has a great influence on a staff's perceptions and attitudes that create organizational climate" (p. 35), and this begins with the manager's style of leadership. Momeni (2009) identified six leadership styles based on different components of emotional intelligence—coercive, authoritative, affiliative, democratic, pacesetting, and coaching (Brackett, Rivers, & Salovey, 2011; Brett, Gulliya, & Crispo, 2012; Goleman, 2001). Of these six styles of leadership, only four "have a positive effect on climate and results" (Goleman, 2001, p. 42). These are the affiliative, democratic, pacesetting, and coaching styles (Table 8-2).

Table 8-2. Four Leadership Styles with Positive Impact on Climate

Leadership Style	Definition	Positive Effects on Climate
Affiliative	Focus on people, team building, bonding, and forging alliances. Useful in creating teams or for healing dysfunctional relationships.	Emotional needs are met.
Democratic	Useful style to adopt when attempting to involve a wide range of people in decision making or building consensus.	Participative. Good and bad is discussed.
Pacesetting	The leader sets the example by working at high levels and standards of performance. Useful to raise the stakes when a competent and motivated team is working well.	Challenging and exciting goals at all levels.
Coaching	Focus on helping to improve people's strengths and building skills to develop managers and future leaders.	Corporate goals are connected to individual goals. Strengths and weaknesses are developed. Career aspirations are put into action.

Source: Adapted with permission from "An EI Theory of Performance," by D. Goleman, In C. Cherniss and D. Goleman (Eds.), *The Emotionally Intelligent Workplace. How to Select for, Measure, and Improve Emotional Intelligence in Individuals, Groups, and Organizations*, 2001, San Francisco, CA: Jossey-Bass, p. 42.

The success of a business today revolves largely around people, not capital (Barber & Strack, 2005; Brackett et al., 2011; Brett et al., 2012). In HPOs, leaders focus on people to build and sustain an excellent organizational environment. These four leadership styles have a positive impact on climate due to the people focus. Of these styles, none is better than the other; in fact, each style is useful in different situations (Rosete & Ciarrochi, 2005). Knowing when to use the appropriate style will help you be a better leader. Excellent leadership is perhaps the most effective way to affect organizational climate and have positive effects on organizational performance.

Chancellor Meyer, at UW–Stout, described in an interview how the leadership style at his institution embodies the people-process culture. "I suspect that the University of Wisconsin–Stout might have been created by James Hoff Stout as a people-process culture . . . , because the culture just seemed to be very people oriented when I came here. . . . It was very evident before books were written on [servant leadership]. I think the people [who] worked here subscribed to that kind of leadership style. That made it a very rewarding place . . . to work as an employee. It made it a very rewarding place to be as a student. I think when employees are engaged and have a focus on student learning and celebrate it, it is very easy for them in whatever role they have at the university to do that . . . If you read the inscription on Bowman Hall, it says something to the effect [of] promoting the learning on skill, industry, and honor. I think that it was very interesting that James Hoff Stout founded the institution to acquire what he needed for his skilled workers. He wanted them to be well-rounded people. That's why the word *honor* shows up in that inscription over at Bowman Hall. He was very interested in creating leaders. I do believe that . . . I think that James Hoff Stout was probably very much a people-process person. I think the way that he established the institution really set it on a course to be a people-process culture type of university" (R. Meyer, personal communication, October 6, 2014).

When a people-process culture leader puts these values into action, people-process culture organizations and their stakeholders (e.g., their employees, vendors, suppliers, and partners) benefit. These values put into action create the organizational climate, which is a relatively enduring characteristic of an organization distinguishing it from other organizations and embodies members' collective perceptions about their organization related to autonomy, trust, cohesiveness, support, recognition, innovation, and fairness (Moran & Volkwein, 1992).

The characteristics of a people-process culture organizational climate are distinct from those of other climates and can be encouraged over the course of an organization's development. If the leaders walk the talk and truly put the value system into action, it will become the very fabric of the organization and will be integral to its success.

Jeffrey Cernohous expanded on the importance of having authentic leadership. "The leadership has to have an open-door policy. The people have to trust those leaders. The leadership has to be able to walk through a plant floor and connect with people. I think authentic leadership is a critical aspect to creating a people culture" (J. Cernohous, personal communication, July 25, 2014).

High-Performance Organizations Exercise the Right Leadership

You have probably heard the adages "people quit their bosses, not their jobs" and "a lost employee is more than a person lost" (Bassi & McMurrer, 2007). In Business School 101, everyone learns that bad management affects the bottom line in many ways, including through turnover. In addition to turnover, less than optimal management practices have a limitless list of negative and costly implications for organizations, including increased absenteeism, decreased productivity, deflated employee morale, high stress, and health issues, to name a few. Bad management can also lead to increased fear, intimidation, and workplace bullying.

Leaders of HPOs promote a healthy organizational culture. Effective leaders know that when employees fear for their jobs or lack job security, they feel powerless and may become intimidated and vulnerable (Sidle, 2009). Leaders of HPOs have zero tolerance for workplace bullying, and they eradicate fear from the work environment.

Not surprising, people-process leaders proactively guard the cultural health of their organizations. They recognize that a lack of alignment or dysfunction in one element will eventually have a negative impact on other areas. The leadership at UW–Stout offers a prime example of the benefits of embracing the people-process culture. As Chancellor Meyer put it, "Chancellor Bob Swanson [my predecessor] was definitely a people-process culture person. . . . He had an amazing capacity to remember people's names or remember something about people, so that the next time he would run into you, . . . he would say, 'Bob, how are you doing and how is the student senate going?' It was remarkable what he remembered about people. He was very invested in developing the person. He was very interested beyond what your interests were and how you were doing. . . . I really think . . . this was really sort of a petri dish for people-process culture development" (R. Meyer, personal communication, October 6, 2014).

The management of trust rests on how the leaders demonstrate consistency (Bennis, 1989; Hennessey, 1998). Leaders who elicit the greatest amount of trust are characterized as keeping their word and as clearly communicating with their staff (Hennessey, 1998; Valentino, 2004). HPOs all share one thing: visionary and dynamic leaders at all levels, from the chief executive officer to the production-floor supervisor, who daily personify and practice the shared corporate values in everything they do and say (Sagiv et al., 2011).

Cernohous, a former mentee of Bob Cervenka, stated, "I was lucky that through my networking I found my way to Bob. So I am fairly passionate about giving back, just like Bob was, to the community. . . . Really, I think the best way to do that is to start new businesses and enterprises. But a key part of that is having the right leadership . . . in place" (J. Cernohous, personal communication, July 25, 2014).

The successful implementation of strategies is aligned with an organizational leader's effectiveness in making decisions, the effective marshaling of resources and capabilities, and appropriate responses to the environment (Connell, 2001). In other words, regardless of a firm's size, its survival will depend on strategic awareness translated into implementable goals, capital, and control systems (Flavel & Williams, 1996). Founded and operated by visionary leaders who believe that making money and treating people right go hand in hand, people-process cultures are known for having a clear, compelling mission and strategic stretch goals that are continually communicated to their employees in multiple forms. Strategic awareness must therefore include self-awareness on the part of the managers, including an awareness of their own management style and its possible influence on employees and the organization's culture (Osborne & Cowen, 2002). By walking the talk, people-process culture leaders at all levels create environments that foster communication, build trust, and facilitate teamwork.

Bob Cervenka was a proponent of authentic communication. "Leadership is practicing respect for people," he said. "Being a good leader means being a very good listener. Leaders communicate the most by walking around the production floor or lab and asking, 'How is it going today? What's going on?'" (Original PPC Handbook, Phillips Plastics Corporation, 1994).

Investing in competent managers can aid in supporting organizational resiliency. A focus on managerial training can help organizations identify and develop effective managers, and ensure they develop the skills they need to clearly communicate the organizational culture to their employees. Training can help managers energize, change, and develop their people—connecting them with learning opportunities and providing coaching and frequent feedback in support of career development (Towers Watson, 2014b). Strategically managing the company's intellectual capacity also means continuing to practice and adopt state-of-the-art technologies and process innovations while creating new knowledge—and business opportunities—through ongoing research and development.

Leaders need to be aware of their actions and how they are interpreted in people-process-based cultures. This awareness and behavior is reflected in and modeled by genuineness, care, and authenticity of the leader and leadership within the organization (Norman, Luthans, & Luthans, 2005).

Leadership, then, is the ability to create and work well with the organization and community to ensure successful connections. People-first organizations have leaders who can read and predict through complexity, think through complex problems, engage groups in dynamic adaptive organizational change, and manage emotion appropriately. In essence, such leadership is the key to how internal and external organizational dynamics translate and link internally to the organization and externally to the community.

Leaders who adopt the people-process culture value system play a critical role in communicating and demonstrating the true importance of a people-process culture to the organization's members. A people-process culture leader puts these values into action. In doing so, people-process culture organizations and their stakeholders benefit.

HPOs will achieve long-term sustained competitiveness and an advantage over rivals by operating under the premise of a people-process organizational philosophy. Organizations that adopt this people-process mindset will foster the diversity of their leaders and, as a result, will experience a more positive, innovative, people-oriented workplace environment.

CHAPTER 9

Finding—and Keeping—
the Right Employees

Winning companies place a premium on recruiting, hiring, and training highly talented people. Hires that are not an organizational fit are costly, so people-centered organizations want to get it right the first time.

Hytter (2007) demonstrated that workplace factors such as rewards, leadership style, career opportunities, training and development of skills, physical working conditions, and work–life balance have an indirect influence on retention. Several other factors also influence employee engagement and retention: the existence of challenging and meaningful work, opportunities for advancement, empowerment, responsibility, managerial integrity and quality, and new opportunities or challenges (Birt, Wallis, & Winternitz, 2004). Walker (2001) also identified seven factors that encouraged retention, which were identified as

1. compensation and appreciation of the work performed,
2. the provision of challenging work,
3. opportunities to learn,
4. positive relationships with colleagues,
5. recognition of capabilities and performance contributions,
6. a good work–life balance, and
7. good communication within the organization.

High-Performance Organizations Exercise the Right Human Resources Practices

Whether an organization is high performing depends on the mental models of its HR team. The mental models that HR professionals form may affect their effectiveness at work, the workplace experiences of their employees, the strategies and practices of their firms, and the professionalism of HR as a strategic partner in the organization (Labedz & Lee, 2011). Pfeffer (2005) suggested that diagnosing and changing mental models held within organizations may be the most important task facing HR. The good news is that the ability to sustain high performance is learnable.

Changing mental models through critical self-reflection on behavior may help HR and leadership build relationships with employees, promote a healthy organizational culture, and avoid costly turnover. HPOs are committed to providing stable work environments for their employees, with equal opportunity for learning, personal growth, and development. They implement this by building relationships and treating their employees with respect and a caring attitude. The leaders and HR professionals of an HPO understand the importance of cultivating healthy environments and developing relationships with their employees, connecting with them, and connecting people to what is important in their own lives.

HPOs also celebrate workplace diversity. They embrace the similarities and differences among their employees in terms of cultural background, physical ability, race, sex, sexual orientation, religion, and age. They know that a lack of diversity limits an organization. Although all considerations of diversity present unique challenges, diversity in the ages of the workforce members is especially challenging, because this is the first time in American history that organizations are dealing with five generations in the workplace: traditionalists, baby boomers, and generations X, Y, and millennials (Table 9-1).

Table 9-1. Multigenerational Workforce

Name	Born	Characteristics
Traditionalists Matures, Pre-Boomers, Veterans	Before 1946	Loyal, consistent, conforming
Baby Boomers	1946–1964	Competitive, political, hardworking
Generation X	1965–1976	Individualistic, disloyal, techno literate
Generation Y Millennials, Nexters	1977–1997	Techno literate, purposed, multitasking
Generation Z Gen 2020, iGeneration, Silent Generation	After 1997	Lack interpersonal skills, rely on World Wide Web and social media for communication, do not believe in career and formal studies, desire instant action and results

Each of the five generations has a different set of values, expectations, and attitudes that have the potential to wreak havoc on productivity, but, when they are leveraged properly, they can increase efficiency, employee morale, and job satisfaction (Kyles, 2005).

Communities of Work

Communities of work tend to behave as flexible networks of people, where the organizational identity provides the glue. Individuals are socialized and identify with these communities of work. People belonging to a community of work permanently face a complex balancing act across four dimensions:

- Organizational values shape the community of work, connect necessary talents to the organization, and provide the groundwork for a specific identity.
- Organizational values also lay the foundation for the organization to function as a societal actor. Organizations that are in a quest to embed corporate social responsibility in their strategy should make these values explicit to all stakeholders.

- Organizational values provide the basis for the continuous creation of social capital, inside and outside the organization.
- Organizational values guide the behavior of employees in their interaction with stakeholders, inside and outside the organization (Metcalf & Benn, 2012).

A satisfying work environment is created through supporting the employees on several fronts: competitive compensation, learning opportunities for career advancement, effective communication, and support of a psychologically healthy environment. An organizational culture aligned with these and other factors will result in happier employees, who will work harder for the company and who will stay with the organization longer. Making the workplace pleasant for both employees and managers can help in employee retention and satisfaction, and this can lead to increased productivity, better communication, and improved profitability. Employees who enjoy their workplace are more open to embracing the corporate culture. They may also be more willing to share it and the company's goals with their colleagues and with customers.

Aligned Operations and Work Environments Focus on Human Resources and Talent Development Practices

In people-process cultures, the corporate structure and design; facilities and architecture; and behind-the-scenes services such as research and development, marketing, accounting, finance, and HR are carefully aligned to support people, relationships, and the process of working together (Osborne & Cowen, 2002).

Kathryn Roberts of Ecumen stated, "We focus a lot on talent development internally. We have a program that identifies about a dozen upcoming leaders every year, and we put them through a . . . rigorous yearlong leadership-development program that ends in an active-learning project. It's not [about] how to do performance reviews [or] how to reset the time clock. It's about how to live with integrity, how to be who you say you are, [and] how to recognize your skills and weaknesses. It's those kinds of activities. And the people . . . we have graduated are just rock stars" (K. Roberts, personal communication, July 9, 2014).

HR plays a vital role in incorporating a value component into practices such as employee selection, appraisal, training and development, compensation, and reward systems (Hassan, 2007). Investing in the human and social capital of employees is critical for today's organizations (Luthans, Vogelgesang, & Lester, 2006). According to Denison (1990), organizations achieve greater effectiveness to the extent that their consistency in translating core values is developed within their HR policies and practices. Enhancing the employability of their employees fosters engagement from those employees, and organizations realize the added benefit of increased commitment and ownership from them as well (Luthans et al., 2006). Successful organizations employ innovative talent development practices to retain and support their employees (Zairi, 1998).

Companies serious about obtaining profits by supporting their people will expend the effort needed to ensure that they recruit the right people in the first place. First, the organization needs to have a large applicant pool from which to select. Second, the organization needs to be clear about what the most critical skills and attributes for the ideal candidate are. Third, the skills and abilities sought must be carefully considered and should be consistent with the particular job requirements and the organization's approach to its market. Fourth, organizations should screen primarily for important attributes that are difficult to change through training and should emphasize the qualities that differentiate the candidates.

After they are hired, employees need strong reward systems and motivators to perform at their full ability and to develop a sense of ownership of the organization. Supervisors and managers must consider the importance of collaboration and sharing best practices when designing reward systems (Martins & Meyer, 2012). Compensation and incentive plans, for example, are tied to department and organizational performance, as well as to individual achievement. Therefore, a real source of competitive advantage is an organization's ability to create conditions that allow its members to experience unconditional trust (Jones & George, 1998). People-process cultures develop processes and systems, from flexible benefits and profit sharing to top-notch training, equipment, and research and development facilities that reflect the organization's core values. Organizations should evaluate the need to reallocate and further differentiate their limited incentive and reward resources to the employee segments that provide the greatest return on investment. Sustained profitable growth requires alignment between the goals and objectives of the employee value proposition and the total rewards strategy of the business. It also requires a culture that attracts and retains the talent with the skills that the organization needs (Towers Watson, 2014b). People-process cultures manage the organization's intellectual and social capital—as well as its ability to listen and respond to customers and employees—as critical factors in developing effective asset and process HR development strategies. These strategies are focused on workforce development practices and smart business strategies that get results.

Dave Lagerstrom believes that buy-in at all levels is important. "We have buy-in from everyone. It has to start at the top. The key is having the right people, doing the right job, with the motivation to do their work to the best of their ability. That runs throughout the organization. . . . When we have a new hire, within a few days of them starting, someone from our HR team will sit down with them and conduct an interview to determine their personal goals. What are they trying to accomplish? . . . We make sure that we are doing the things that they need and the things that they are interested in learning and growing in their career. The interesting thing is that specifically with the high potential people we have identified, we have been able to keep them in the company even though they want to change roles. So this means finding a completely different role in a different department and giving them those opportunities. Our voluntary turnover is currently less than two percent, in an industry that is averaging somewhere between eleven and fifteen percent. It's a huge, huge cost driver over time. If you consider the knowledge that walks out the door when you have an employee leave and the cost to replace them. With all of our high potential employees we conduct annual interviews just to understand where they are in their career and in their development. We find out what things we can do for them, what educational opportunities or different role, and [we make] sure that we meet those needs" (D. Lagerstrom, personal communication, September 3, 2014).

Organizational support requires the organizational culture to encourage new opportunities. It necessitates cooperation between departments to allow those employees who share a passion to embrace it (Martins & Meyer, 2012). In people-process cultures, the traditional corporate command and control barriers of hierarchy, rank, and status are replaced by processes and work environments that encourage, recognize, and reward teamwork, flexibility, and innovation—essential elements for competing successfully in today's tough global markets.

Meaningful Work

Many employees today want to work for an organization that embraces and engages them as a whole person—work that gives the employees life purpose and leaders who provide them with a clear purpose. Specifically, employees want to make decisions and perform work that is meaningful and psychologically rewarding and that helps fulfill their emotional and social needs (Sisodia et al., 2014). People are often not fully engaged at work, because they don't get to make meaningful decisions (Bakke, 2013). This dissatisfaction is not uncommon; trust in others' ability to make meaningful decisions is rare (Bakke, 2013, p. 203). The employees of HPOs know their work has inherent value and will positively affect the lives of others. This is demonstrated through HPO systems that are structured to reward employees for positive contributions to their organization and to the broader community and for being responsible global citizens. These employees gain deep satisfaction from their work.

People-process culture companies plant the seed for future profits and long-term survival by reinvesting resources and profits back into the business. They want to make sure their people have the best possible tools available to meet tomorrow's demands. This ability to develop long-term financial strategies is one of the major characteristics that differentiates people-process culture companies from the rest of industry.

The people-process culture, with its emphasis on people, teamwork, and creativity, offers rich opportunities for growing new high-tech firms. In people-process cultures, business strategies and tactics combine with people skills to make innovation possible. People-first companies engage in continuous improvement and rigorous preventive maintenance programs by replacing and updating equipment on a continuous cycle. State-of-the-art equipment and facilities are hallmarks of a true people-process culture. Giving people the best tools available to get the job done places a premium on those people and on their performance.

Pay Tied to Company Performance

Money matters. People-first companies are willing to pay for results, tying compensation to individual, team, and organizational performance. Contingent compensation also figures importantly in most high-performance work systems. Such compensation can take a number of different forms, including gain sharing, profit sharing, stock ownership, payment for skill, or various forms of individual team incentives (Pfeffer & Veiga, 1999).

Chancellor Meyer, at UW–Stout, discussed the idea of rewarding success: "So another aspect of the people-process culture and good servant leadership is that you celebrate success often. Try to reward people by saying thank you. I think it's in the book *The Heart of a Leader* by Ken Blanchard. He has a quote in there that I love: He says try catching people doing something right. I just love that quote, because it is the opposite focus of continuous improvement. It's sort of the opposite side of that. Let's catch you doing something right and celebrate it. That's the people-process culture" (R. Meyer, personal communication, October 6, 2014).

People-process cultures make sure that all people benefit from the company's success. They believe that all stakeholders—employees, customers, suppliers, vendors, shareholders, owners, and community members—should reap the benefits of the company's success. Such compensation can take a number of different forms, including gain sharing, profit sharing, stock ownership, payment for skills, and various forms of individual team incentives. This sharing gives the employees a sense of ownership in the company, and when employees are own-ers, they act and think like owners (Pfeffer & Veiga, 1999). By tying compensation to individual, business unit, and overall company per-formance, people-process cultures give people a genuine stake in the financial health of the enterprise and in the process of working together. Employees who see a direct correlation between their day-to-day per-formance and their paycheck tend to be more highly motivated, pro-ductive, and cost conscious.

Employees differ in how they experience and interpret the HR practices by which they are managed (Nishii, Lepak, & Schnei-der, 2008), and high-performance HR systems rely on the creation of mutual investment-based employment relationships and positive mutual social exchange (Kehoe & Wright, 2013). Common among high-performance HR systems is a focus on the consistency of employ-ees' performance behaviors with organizational goals with respect to promoting on the basis of ability, motivation, and opportunity (Kehoe & Wright, 2013).

A focus on the growth and development of its people and the establishment of strong foundations of trust and communication are the hallmarks of high-performance people-process cultures. Gone are the days when product design, production process, or customer service could create a competitive advantage. It is the skills and abil-ities of individual employees that dictate the future of the organiza-tion. To address this fact, the organization must ensure that its staff are challenged and suitably rewarded, and today we see organizations offering attractive benefit packages, including childcare and a host of other benefits.

Reduced Status Distinctions

In order to help make all organizational members feel important and committed, most high-performance management systems attempt to reduce the status distinctions that separate the levels of hierarchy and that cause some people to feel less valued (Pfeffer & Veiga, 1999). This is accomplished in two principal ways: symbolically, through the use of language and labels, physical space, and dress, and substantively, in reducing of the organization's degree of wage inequality, particularly among levels. People-first cultures proactively work against typical corporate caste systems, minimizing differences among wages, benefits, job titles, dress, language, parking, and office arrangements.

Employment Security

Loyalty has its price, but long-term benefits outweigh short-term gains. People who aren't worried about when the next corporate ax will fall can focus on making a product, keeping customers happy, and creating new opportunities.

Employment security can be counterproductive unless the firm hires people who fit the culture and unless incentives reward outstanding performance. Implementing work teams will not accomplish much unless the teams receive training in specific technical skills and team processes and are given financial and operating performance goals and information (Pfeffer & Veiga, 1999). People-process cultures believe fervently in providing all workers with long-term employment security.

Work–Life Balance

People-process companies also stress balance between work, home, and community life. Team leaders don't view their people as anonymous cogs in the great corporate wheel; they know and care about each individual and his or her family. But leaders in people-process culture companies have an even greater respect for their people. Sometimes, the most important job a people-process culture leader will ever perform is to make sure his or her people go home at the end of the day.

A talented workforce brings innovation and creativity that increase the overall effectiveness of the organization. Recruiting the best talent doesn't happen overnight. Developing game-changing, people-first talent strategies begins with establishing an HR system that leverages the right human capital by acquiring, developing, and motivating the very best talent (Posthuma, Campion, Masimova, & Campion, 2013), including connectors. HPOs that exercise the right leadership, HR practices, and talent management strategies may gain an advantage over their competitors.

CHAPTER 10

Lifelong Learning and Professional Development

People-first organizations require an educated workforce to make their system function. They leverage learning by creating learning opportunities for growth and create an organized process to support employees in doing exceptional work (Holder, 1994). Learning drives performance and innovation in the information age. Top companies invest heavily in ongoing training and education for all people (Pfeffer & Veiga, 1999).

Knowledge and skill are critical, and too few organizations act on this insight. Training is an essential component of high-performance work systems because these systems rely on frontline employee skill and initiative to identify and resolve problems, to initiate changes in work methods, and to take responsibility for quality. Training is an investment in the organization's staff, in the current business climate, and virtually begs for some sort of return-on-investment calculations. The fundamental premise of high-performance management systems is that organizations perform at a higher level when they are able to tap the ideas, skill, and effort of all their people (Pfeffer & Veiga, 1999). All of this requires a skilled and motivated workforce that has the knowledge and capability to perform the requisite tasks. Training can be a source of competitive advantage in numerous industries for firms with the wisdom to use it (Pfeffer & Veiga, 1999).

By nurturing individual and organizational learning, people-process cultures are actively shaping their own futures. The more eager an employee is to learn, and the more creative solutions he uses, the more likely he is to stay working in the organization (Govaerts, Kyndt, Dochy, & Baet, 2011). Talent leads to exceptional performance, and talented employees are often admired and valued.

Chancellor Meyer, at UW–Stout, spoke to the importance of creating a forward-looking culture. "You want to establish your organization as a learning organization. What you're doing there is setting up a culture for growing. I don't think most people want to be employed in an organization that is not forward looking and thinking about developing its people and their growth. So that's why measurement is important to make sure that people are growing. You know, what I look for in people is honesty and openness. Celebrate that: hard work, smart work, and commitment—a team approach" (R. Meyer, personal communication, October 6, 2014).

The most powerful learning is generally experiential in nature, and return-on-investment benefits should accrue during (as well as after) the course of the learning activity, especially if the learner implements his or her own solutions and tracks the outcomes using both "hard" and "soft" measures that are relevant to the project's implementation and evaluation. Table 10-1 describes the five levels of learning effectiveness.

Table 10-1. Five Levels for
Evaluating Learning Effectiveness

Level	Category	Description	Techniques
1	Reaction	Learning is subjectively reviewed by the learner on completion. Learners give their personal views and impressions of the relative value added	Learning transfer questionnaire
2	Learning	Evaluates the learning journey in terms of key insights, experiences, and outcomes	Learning transfer questionnaire
3	Job behavior	Reviews ways in which the action learning course affected the learner's work performance (6–9 months later)	Structured interviews
4	Organization	Considers the overall impact of the courses on the organization, using criteria such as productivity and labor turnover	Impact on guest satisfaction survey, labor turnover, and staff satisfaction survey statistics
5	ROI level	Assesses the impact of learning on profitability and growth of the organization as a whole	Investment appraisal techniques

Source: Adapted with permission from "High Performance Learning at Work," by R. Teare, H. Ingram, G. Prestoungrage, and E. Sandelands, 2002, *International Journal of Contemporary Hospitality Management, 14*(7), p. 379. Adapted with permission. Copyright 2002 by Emerald Group Publishing.

Learning helps employees achieve their highest levels of performance and engagement. It is a vital investment in the future and makes strategic sense. Continuous learning is a reality that needs to be managed and facilitated so it positively affects the business's bottom line.

Echols (2007) stated that, when combined with selective promotion and salary action, the learning and development process is a strong retention activity. A review of the literature reveals that learning and development opportunities appear crucial for the retention of talented employees (Arnold, 2005; Echols, 2007; Hytter, 2007; Rodriguez, 2008; Walker, 2001).

Ulrich (2008) argued that talent can help turn objectives into actions through the consideration of three elements: competence, commitment, and contribution. In today's knowledge economy, learning is essential for knowledge creation and creating a global competitive advantage (Scaringella & Malaeb, 2014). If employees keep learning and are flexible, they can direct their own futures, and the opportunities and working conditions they desire can be open to them.

Talent is something that penetrates the entire company and is therefore never exclusively connected to one function. Talented employees are creative and committed to their work, meaning they are naturally innovative. Therefore, they are able to generate new processes, new products, and even new markets (Scaringella & Malaeb, 2014).

A company must consider the added value of every employee, and not only the value of those who occupy top positions (Govaerts et al., 2011). Providing education, training, and development for all employees is a necessity. According to Mele (2003), an inconsistent approach to development can not only diminish loyalty but also increase insecurity even more than layoffs, thus further eroding employee commitment. Organizations must establish supportive learning and working climates. Accredited action learning provides the mechanism for open-minded organizations to review their learning and development strategy, offering opportunities to employees at every level of the organization.

Organizations train their employees because they want to develop more skilled and knowledgeable workers. The professionals hired to perform the training can help organizations stay focused, using coaching, and a strategic approach to training creates workplace innovation and change (Miller, 2010).

Brad Wucherpfennig spoke in our interview about the importance of training his workers. "Our first alignment is to make sure that the coworker knows how to do the job, how to do the job safely, and that he is given the right tools to do the job. . . . There is training [that] gets into talent development. They learn those things. Some of our people start in the craft. We send them to college; they become civil engineers. They come back and work as project managers. We see a lot of that" (B. Wucherpfennig, personal communication, August 5, 2014).

Corporate trainers can provide on-site and e-learning workshops and training tailored to meet the specific needs and interests of various business units. However, Wainright (1997) recommended that train- ing also be developed to help employees become better people to assist with developing interpersonal skills and the ability to manage conflict, which would foster increased employee engagement. Learning can be designed and leveraged to meet certification requirements for the rel- evant industry or continuing education credits for licensure.

Career Path and Planning

Career planning and opportunities to advance in the organization have been found to be directly related to retention (Chen, Wang, & Chu, 2010). Given the reported shortage of skilled and talented employees across diversified industries, the trend and research point to a criti- cal HR management issue. Although career management started off as a means of addressing individual employees' career needs, it has slowly evolved into a mechanism by which the organization provides tools, resources, and structure so that employees are able to assess and develop themselves and create plans within the context of organiza- tional realities (Krishnan & Maheshwari, 2011).

People-process culture organizations are readily aware of this reality and strongly encourage mentoring and career paths for all employees. Therefore, recognition and acknowledgment of the skills and abilities that employees have gained since joining the organization may make them eligible for the next level of advancement. A career ladder chart leveraged as organizational road maps can facilitate the career development discussion. Mentoring programs also can facilitate career coaching and the career paths of employees. The goal is to focus on the potential human capital of the employee, not just those skills and abilities that they possessed when they were first hired. Promoting from within can also decrease recruitment and retention costs and should therefore be encouraged. Career path planning and development allows employees the ability to map out their personal journey to the future with the assistance of a trusted guide already invested in the culture and success of the organization.

Tuition Reimbursement and Educational Assistance

Another mechanism to foster a continuous learning environment is through tuition reimbursement or educational assistance programs. In today's knowledge economy, where there is an ongoing war for talent, it is important for organizations to create an environment where employees can pursue both personal and professional goals (Champion-Hughes, 2001). Tuition reimbursement for the completion of college or technical courses that pertain to any current or future position at the company may be useful. This has been found to be beneficial for both the employee and employer. Employees can pursue personal and learning goals to enhance their learning and development. Employers benefit by being able to leverage the skills and knowledge acquired by the employee (Champion-Hughes, 2001).

Brad Wucherpfennig shared his definition of success in our interview: "I would deem success [as] having an educated, trained workforce ready to take on new challenges in the marketplace. You will always have competition. You need to be able to serve the customer's needs, including being closer to the customer, applying the same principles to the customers as well as the supply base. I would define success as an energized workforce seeking new challenges and meeting the customers' needs" (B. Wucherpfennig, personal communication, August 5, 2014).

People-first organizations also partner with area technical colleges and universities to provide top-notch training and curriculum, creating customized instruction opportunities for employees. One of the goals of such programs is to foster student competency that enables companies to develop more advanced relationships with customers and suppliers (Ricks & Williams, 2005). This process also allows for the creation of integrated work environments that create career paths for employees. This is a win–win for all parties (employees, companies, and technical colleges or universities).

Debbie Cervenka shared how Phillips encouraged its employees to grow their careers, "Well I guess . . . we did that in a variety of ways . . . We put learning centers in all of our facilities. . . . We actually supported people's desire to take courses outside of the company through education assistance. We promoted within whenever possible. All jobs, probably with the exception of very top-level executive positions, were posted in the company. People saw where opportunities existed and . . . what was required . . . to better themselves" (D. Cervenka, personal communication, July 29, 2014).

Internships and Cooperative Education Opportunities

Strategic corporate philanthropy practices and partnerships are designed to develop performance-ready talent for the workforce (Ricks

& Williams, 2005). People-first organizations provide on-the-job learning to soon-to-be and new graduates to ensure a more successful school-to-work transition by introducing them to the people-process culture and way of doing business. Companies can only succeed in the long term if they recruit and motivate highly skilled people who are able to respond to and shape the challenges of the future (Greening & Turban, 2000). Effective recruitment is crucial to the development of a cohesive workforce and a successful organization.

Recruitment directly affects the quality of a potential applicant pool (Frank, Finnegan, & Taylor, 2004). As is the case at Baker Concrete and Construction, individuals who participate in these types of positions are often offered permanent employment before the close of their internship or co-op. Brad Wucherpfennig said, "We have a big intern and co-op program. They come and see the nature of the work. Some college students may be with us four summers, before they are hired on as project engineer. We try to align them when they are trained in the field" (B. Wucherpfennig, personal communication, August 5, 2014).

Chancellor Meyer, at UW–Stout, stated, "Developing people professionally takes longer than developing them for a semester of class. It was very, very enriching and rewarding for me to be able to accomplish what my predecessors had done. . . . That's why I went on the path that I did. I think that Stout . . . has been very blessed by having great leaders who believe in the people-process culture. So it's endemic already in the culture. It is easy to carry it on. People understand it. They want it" (R. Meyer, personal communication, October 6, 2014).

CHAPTER 11

Organizational Resiliency

An HPO is a learning organization, and according to Wilhelm (2006), learning organizations compete better in the marketplace because they have superior brand equity and can attract and retain the best talent. But, what is a learning organization? It "is a collective entity [that] focuses on the question of 'what'; that is, what are the characteristics of an organization such that it (represented by all members) may learn?" (Yeo, 2005, p. 369).

As with other terms discussed in this book, there is very little consensus as to what constitutes a learning organization. Table 11-1 captures the variety of definitions and themes that theorists use when explaining the concept.

Table 11-1. Thematic and Definitional Landscape of Learning Organizations

Theorist	Theme	Definition
Argyris (1993)	Theory in action	In a learning organization, individuals are the key where they are acting in order to learn, or where they are acting to produce a result. All the knowledge has to be generalized and crafted in ways in which the mind and brain can use it in order to make it actionable.
Emery (1993)	Organizational structure and design	A learning organization is one that is "structured in such a way that its members can learn and continue to learn within it" (p. 2).

Continued

Theorist	Theme	Definition
Garratt (1995)	Action learning	A learning organization is linked to action learning processes where it releases the energy and learning of the people in the hour-to-hour, day-to-day operational cycle of business.
Marquardt & Kearsley (1999)	Technological	A learning organization has the powerful capacity to collect, store, and transfer knowledge and thereby continuously transform itself for corporate success. It empowers people within and outside the company to learn as they work. A most critical component is the utilization of technology to optimize both learning and productivity.
Pedler, Burgoyne, & Boydell (1991)	Growth and survival	A learning organization is like a fountain tree where the image of energy and life is characteristic of growth and survival. Organizational members are constituents of this fountain tree.
Watkins & Marsick (1993)	Team building	A learning organization is one that learns continuously and transforms itself where the organizational capacity for innovation and growth is constantly enhanced.
Yeo (2005)	Organizational characteristics	A learning organization "is a collective entity which focuses on the question of 'what'; that is, what are the characteristics of an organization such that it (represented by all members) may learn" (p. 369).

Source: Adapted from "Revisiting the Roots of Learning Organization: A Synthesis of the Learning Organization Literature," by R. K. Yeo, 2005, The Learning Organization, 12(4), pp. 368–382. Adapted with permission.

Furthermore, Kirkman, Lowe, and Young (1999) from the Center of Creative Leadership identified eight characteristics of a learning organization, which are listed here:

1. These organizations tend to learn what they value (e.g., quality, efficiency, bureaucracy, customers).
2. A systemic rather than a functional approach to learning is preferred (i.e., learning with strategic intent).
3. They encourage a structured methodology or a forum for cross-functional dialogue that does not crumble to operational or financial pressures to reallocate human capital.

4. Learning organizations focus on understanding parameters and scenarios rather than on optimizing solutions.
5. They view learning as a process (journey) rather than an outcome (destination).
6. They create learning forums with explicit goals in mind.
7. They develop systems for the fast and efficient transfer of information.
8. They embed the reasons for organizational successes or failures in the collective organizational memory (Kirkman et al., 1999, p. 6).

This diverse range of conceptualizations aside, one of the key challenges facing leaders remains the effective implementation of learning within their organizations, partly because of a gap between principles and practices and partly because of the lack of an enabling, people-focused organizational culture.

Companies with people-process cultures are constantly seeking new knowledge and new ways to apply what they already know to improve their processes, products, and services. Staying on the leading edge of change requires significant investments in research and development. Strategic partnerships and early involvement with customers are process innovations that help companies get it right the first time. People-process culture organizations are always looking for new products that probably are not manufactured yet. This out-of-the-box thinking and management style can create organizational chaos but, at the same time, promotes innovation and strategic thinking.

Kathryn Roberts spoke in our interview about how she and her employees encourage innovation within the people-process culture: "It takes a long time. It takes perseverance. You have to have a hard shell. You can't be running a popularity contest. You have to have your eye on the outcomes that you are looking for and not waver. . . . You need to have a really trusted team, . . . a group of people with diverse styles, . . . and you really have to respect your brand promise. Our brand promise is that we honor people, we empower, and we innovate. . . . We are doing this really cool thing where we . . . got an instructor from a local university, in St. Paul, who does a 100-day course on how to be an innovator. You start with an idea, and 100 days later, you have to have a business plan. So we did our first class [for the employees of our company], and they loved it" (K. Roberts, personal communication, July 9, 2014).

People-based core values help build cultural systems that allow an organization to adapt to, facilitate, and create change, which makes these cultures and organizations more resilient (Norman et al., 2005). A high-performance people-process culture is able to galvanize its customers, suppliers, employees, and other key stakeholders to reduce threats and to capitalize better on opportunities.

Alignment, motivation, organization, and control can help performance, but only if the resulting actions fit an intelligent business strategy for the specific environment in which the firm operates. In a people-process culture, managing the organization's intellectual capital—its shared knowledge and its ability to listen and respond to its customers and its people—is a critical factor in developing effective work groups and smart business strategies.

Charlie Krueger described change as a necessary part of an organization: "Change is a way of doing business. . . . Change doesn't happen, unless you can respond to change. You can't respond to change unless you have people [who] are aware [of] what the changes are and the kind of moves they have to make at the operational level, the mid-level management, and upper-level management. So if you have to force change all the way down, all the time, before it's accepted or force it on people, the responsiveness is going to be slow. If people are open and willing and part of the business plan, they are part of the organization. You have a culture that allows information to flow back and forth. You are going to pick up on signals sooner. You are going to be able to react sooner. That is going to put you at a business advantage" (C. Krueger, personal communication, July 31, 2014).

Wucherpfennig also believes that adaptability is crucial to having a sustainable HPO. He added, "I think . . . the ability to respond to change ties to people-process culture, because we believe in using the people on the jobs to come up with ideas providing innovation, different ways of doing their job, and develop[ing] their community. So we are really empowering them to deal with their jobsite. Change will come on their jobsite. [It] can come from the ground up or from the top down" (B. Wucherpfennig, personal communication, August 5, 2014).

Organizational resiliency is the capacity of an organization to respond to and even prosper from negative circumstances (Luthans et al., 2006, p. 30). Many corporate leaders have used today's fast-paced business environment and the need to stay nimble as justification for massive layoffs, a heavy use of temporary or contract workers, skyrocketing executive compensation, and the elimination of employment security. Organizational resiliency is important for these leaders for continuous improvement and success in today's marketplace while avoiding measures such as massive layoffs. The ability of leaders to convey the message of hope in the change process to employees results in a significant organizational resiliency and capacity for change in organizations.

"Achieving competitive success through people involves fundamentally altering how we think about the workforce and the employment relationship," Pfeffer (1998) wrote. "It means achieving success by working *with* people, not by replacing them or limiting the scope of activities. It entails seeing the workforce as a source of strategic advantage, not just as a cost to be minimized or avoided" (p. 16).

Hope includes not only the will but also the way to accomplish a goal and a viable plan to accomplish the task (Norman et al., 2005). The leader's level of hope in the face of change encourages the employees of an organization to see the company through crisis and change, affecting the resiliency of the employees and the organization at large. Leaders need to be aware of their actions and how they are interpreted and modeled. This is reflected in employees' reactions to the genuineness, care, and authenticity of the leader (Norman et al., 2005).

The size of the organization can have a significant impact on how it reacts to change. Smaller organizations are frequently able to incorporate strategic management principles over the short term because of simple organizational structures that enable flexibility, facilitate communication, and reduce reactions to change (Flavel & Williams, 1996). Conversely, larger organizations require detailed plans to communicate the goals of the larger organization to its employees. This can lead to a lack of flexibility, speed, and reduced responsiveness to the external environment (Connell, 2001). People-first companies invest heavily in their people and in organizational learning by providing extensive, ongoing communication and rich opportunities for technical training, professional development, education, career planning, and growth. Keeping individual business units small also facilitates agility in the people process. This is done for two strategic reasons: (1) to maintain the people-first culture and sense of community and (2) to develop highly focused business units with unique capabilities to serve a variety of mainstream and niche markets.

According to Pfeffer and Veiga (1999), HPOs share seven people-first characteristics that lead to organizational resiliency:

1. employment security,
2. selective hiring,

3. teamwork and decentralization,
4. pay tied to company performance,
5. extensive training,
6. reduced status distinctions, and
7. open communication.

The adaptive nature of people-process culture organizations consistently and substantially outperforms companies with more traditional corporate cultures in the areas of employee engagement, revenue, workforce development, stock price, and net income.

Flexibility and a willingness to embrace change are hallmarks of a people-process culture. People-process companies encourage people to share ideas, pool resources, and work together to solve common problems. Trust, invention, and innovation flourish in the open organizational climates and environments these cultures create. Employees are encouraged to experiment with unconventional business practices and to test and develop new technology, ideas, and products.

CHAPTER 12

Responsible Global Citizenship

HPOs comprise globally responsible citizens who think critically and act wisely to advance the common good by responding to a wide range of stakeholders. Indeed, employees and organizations may start out by focusing on serving their own interests but evolve over time to serve purposes that transcend mere survival and self-interest. HPOs lead the way in corporate social responsibility. The stakeholders of these organizations adopt new corporate social responsibility values, apply new leadership styles, learn new skills, design more effective decision-making methods, and structure their organization accordingly (van Marrewijk, 2004).

Leslie Lagerstrom, former vice president of marketing for Phillips Plastics Corporation, shared in an interview what the people-process culture was like for her at Phillips. There was a "dedication to local philanthropy and support of local communities. Employees were given time to interact with local communities to do activities, such as coordinate a walk for cancer. . . . This developed a sense of pride in working for Phillips" (L. Lagerstrom, personal communication, June 26, 2014).

Van Marrewijk (2004) found that, to enhance organizational performance, corporations need to focus on their social dimensions. This means that they need to strive to align both the individual and the collective interests of their employees, and the employees need to match their values, personal drivers, capacities, and ambitions with those of the workplace environment. "The alignment of personal and collective interests has become essential to contemporary business. No longer can companies treat their employees as resources, as numbers, as costs, but as human beings" (van Marrewijk, 2004, p. 136). Employees should not be thought of as assets or liabilities but, rather, as human beings, who have social needs.

Debbie Cervenka, former executive vice president of Phillips Plastics Corporation, stated in a 2014 interview, "When the company was small, Bob [Cervenka, cofounder of Phillips] used to literally go into every plant, go into every shift, and hold shift meetings. . . . He would [share company financials] and how the facilities [were] performing. . . . They had to have plant meetings, shift meetings on a monthly basis. We had what we called an open-door policy. . . . We encouraged people to go to their supervisor first and try to work the situation out [to] get [their] question answered. But management also understood—clearly understood—that if the manager wasn't solving that individual's problem, that individual had the right to go to whomever they felt comfortable with. Many of those conversations . . . certainly went to Bob. They went to me. They went to other leaders in the company. People felt empowered . . . that [they could go elsewhere] . . . to seek that information, . . . so that foundation is respecting people, respecting what they do. Understanding that everything that happens in that manufacturing setting is interconnected. . . . So . . . every position was valued. [Only customers had] . . . assigned parking spaces, . . . [so] if you were the CEO and you got there late, you might be in the back of the parking lot. . . . So just that sense of *we are all in this together* and rewarding people based on that. . . . The president's profit percentage was no different [from that of] the person putting the boxes together and taking them to the molding machine. Bob never took a cash bonus when we had cash bonus[es] . . . So if everybody got a three-percent bonus at the end of the year, everybody got a three-percent bonus except for Bob" (D. Cervenka, personal communication, July 29, 2014).

This is critical. Because employees have increasing access to social media, they are more capable than ever of building up their organization's reputation or destroying it (Erb, 2011). HPOs understand this and strive to inspire brand advocacy in their employees through the people-first philosophy and by placing meaning into their work. Deeply ingrained in the culture of an HPO is the belief that everyone is extraordinary and capable of performing astonishing work. This philosophy drives innovative people practices like empowerment, embracing the whole person, corporate social responsibility, brand advocacy, and more. Furthermore, engaging and collaborating with employees and stakeholder groups mandate new social skills within the organization.

Organizational Ethics and Moral Fitness

Cultures that do not espouse a people-oriented focus tend to be obsessed with short-term gains as opposed to long-term success. They hire and retain slash-and-burn leaders that view people as operating costs to be eliminated or restructured or as easily replaceable commodities. Status, ego, ingrained management behaviors, shareholder pressure, ethical lapses, greed, resistance to change, fear, control, poor processes, and system alignment all play a role in this leadership style (Giberson et al., 2009).

Organizational cultures can also be classified as either ethical or unethical, which can be described through the company's policies, procedures, operating principles, and training (Schein, 2010). For example, an artifact of an ethical culture may be a formal code of ethics or a business code of conduct that is based on conducting business honestly. Companies that invest in instilling ethical principles in their organizational culture demonstrate a strong commitment to their organizational values, empowerment, and trust. Ethics provides standards in an organizational culture and the framework for decision making (Schein, 2010). However, the top leaders must model ethical behavior and must show high levels of trust and respect to their fellow members of the culture. Training provides the mechanism for employees to internalize the company's ethics into their daily roles. Along with the trust and respect factors, strong organizational cultures with high ethical standards provide external confidential reporting mechanisms for addressing ethical violations (Giberson et al., 2009).

Ongoing advances in technology are turning ethics into a high-stakes issue for business leaders. They need better ways to help people think through ethical issues and decisions, especially those "right versus right" dilemmas that pit one moral choice against another. Corporate culture and ethics represent a powerful decision-making tool.

Chancellor Meyer, at UW–Stout, stated, "I think . . . the cornerstone has . . . to be honesty. There are a lot of things that you have to do that sometimes challenge your ethics. Being an ethical leader is as important as role modeling ethical decisions. I think being forthright and transparent is important. But having honesty and integrity is a cornerstone to being a good people-process culture person. If you look at the core values that the university has, it really talks about serving a campus community" (R. Meyer, personal communication, October 6, 2014).

Employees at all levels need to develop a greater degree of ethical and moral fitness. The recognition of the common dignity and rights of every person implies an essential equality. Each person is unique, unrepeatable, and different from others. Recognizing these essential qualities of equality, dignity, uniqueness, and diversity is central to a people-process culture.

Another characteristic of every human being is sociability, the capacity to associate and participate in social life. Most people recognize the capacity for the personal growth of human beings, including different aspects such as physical, logical, aesthetic, and moral growth. This shared belief in the dignity of every person and the capacity for personal growth, especially through the acquisition of virtues, is a basic feature of people-process cultures.

In order to achieve a people-process culture, it makes sense to include the management of business toward the common good as one of the features for an organizational humanizing culture instead of the management of business exclusively for profits, power, or any other particular interest if those are contrary to the common good. Caring for people and a sense of service generates loyalty. To summarize, recognition and respect for people and their human rights, care, service, and management toward the common good must be shared beliefs and values in a people-process culture. Management must demonstrate genuine care for their employees. Respecting people and their human rights also means integrity, with a steadfast attitude of trustfulness, keeping promises and fulfilling contacts, fairness, and organizational justice. In other words, people assist, support, and compete with one another through care and service (Grisez & Shaw, 1998, p. 54).

Leslie Lagerstrom said in our interview that, at Phillips Plastics, she expected the same level of commitment and respect from her vendors as she did her employees. "In marketing, we had to reeducate vendors [so they would understand that] we do business with people who do business like we do" (L. Lagerstrom, personal communication, June 26, 2014). Leslie, in her role as VP of marketing, would not tolerate disrespectful references to competitors and called vendors out on it. Sometimes, it meant not doing business with them or getting them to adopt a respectful way of talking about business.

Corporate Social Responsibility and Sustainability

Russell, Haigh, and Griffiths (2007) determined that there are four distinct understandings of sustainability in organizations. Managers described sustainability in terms of

1. a corporation working toward long-term economic performance,
2. a corporation working toward positive outcomes for the natural environment,
3. a corporation that supports employees and social outcomes, or
4. a corporation with a holistic approach to conducting business within a community.

Doing business is no longer only making profits; organizations also have to behave in a socially responsible way. This responsibility includes not only environmental concerns, such as minimizing the organization's carbon footprint, but also must be expanded to include social system issues and international economic issues that must be highly integrated into the organization (Metcalf & Benn, 2012). This quest for new and expanding responsibilities—often called *corporate social responsibility*—implies taking into account issues beyond the conventional scope of a business.

Corporate social responsibility refers to a growing appeal asking organizations to take a broader social responsibility into account, behaving accordingly in an accountable manner, thus behaving as good corporate citizens (Schoemaker et al., 2006). Roome (1992) further suggested that organizational change is embraced and that an ethical approach to work be developed among all employees for organizational sustainability. In this way, employees become the sustainability champions for the company and the community. This is a characteristic of people-process organizations. The main focus of corporate social responsibility is defining the corporate identity, making the company more transparent, and trying to develop a system of accounting for one's actions (Driscoll & Hoffman, 2000). Such linkage is a powerful mediator for successful implementation of sustainability or may even be an expression of it (Metcalf & Benn, 2012).

The sustainable people-process organization can be described as one that reflects the definition of the sustainable organization as those organizations that build on natural capital, enhance human and societal welfare, and contribute to appropriate economic and technological development (Russell & McIntosh, 2011). These companies are innovative and people focused. Sustainability principles are embedded across the organization and within every aspect of the organizational culture. This is the manner in which people-process culture leaders conduct business through the adoption of long-term perspectives that support their employees, business, and communities.

Leslie Lagerstrom shared how Phillips strove to create a sustainable people-process culture: "We need[ed] to do more. [We couldn't] rest on our laurels. The tenets of [people-process culture] need to be fostered on a daily basis. We could never communicate too much. [We were] always looking for what's next . . . [This] had to be nurtured constantly" (L. Lagerstrom, personal communication, June 26, 2014).

The responsible organization can be seen as an organization trying to develop itself as an open system, based on its values and combining market orientation and social responsibility in an indivisible yet distinctive way. Determining which corporate social responsibility activities companies should carry out and which demands and expectations of the society should be taken into account is paramount. Accordingly, an organization is responsible to multiple stakeholders. Corporate social responsibility includes the economics, legal, ethical, and philanthropic responsibility of an organization derived from the claims of its various stakeholders (Lis, 2012). Sustainability programs can provide a vehicle for engaging current and new employees (Boudreau & Ramstad, 2005; Montiel, 2008).

Debbie Cervenka commented on the importance of giving back to the community. "Bob and Louie started the Ann Marie Foundation in 1974 as a way to give back . . . I think . . . the first contribution was like $500, which doesn't sound like a lot today, but it was probably a whole lot more in 1974. Today the foundation is worth approximately $7 million of invested money. . . . It was important to us that the communities that helped Phillips Plastics grow were the ones that would retain the benefits of the success of the company. That's one of the bylaws—that the money has to be distributed within the communities that were home to Phillips Plastics people when we owned the company" (D. Cervenka, personal communication, July 29, 2014).

Companies with a thriving people-process culture care about the communities they do business with. Recognizing that strong communities help support a people-process culture, they believe in giving generously of their time, talents, and financial resources. People-first companies give employees time off to volunteer in neighborhood schools, to collect clothing for needy children, to support recycling and conservation efforts, and so on. Giving back means more than just writing a check. People-process cultures urge their people to get actively involved in community activities. Pledging commitment, personal involvement, and financial support, the company wants to provide lifelong learning opportunities for all of its people and to improve the ability of school systems to produce technically competent and people-oriented graduates.

Chancellor Meyer, at UW–Stout, shared how his graduates are entering the workforce with a more people-centered focus. "It's amazing when you have a culture that has good values, and they have imparted those on our students that leave here. How proud they are when they come back. I'm starting to do frequent alumni events— much more frequently than I ever have. The alumni from this institution are so incredibly appreciative of what we taught them while they were here. What they learned. It's all because I think we are a very effective people-process culture. We have transformed their lives. They are not bashful about sharing that with us. It's a pretty neat thing. It's quite an honor and privilege for me to be able to hear that" (R. Meyer, personal communication, October 6, 2014).

Organizations that make a difference have a passionate and committed staff and are more likely to be driven by values and to have high levels of trust throughout the organization (Weymes, 2005). Inspired employees embrace the organization's core values, as is illustrated in this quotation from Kathryn Roberts. "If you are a maintenance worker and you're in an assisted living building, you will see it when someone is struggling with plugging their lamp in, . . . and the maintenance worker says, 'I have this really good idea for a . . . clever outlet. . . . We could move [it] six feet up the wall and your cord won't show. I will just put it in for you.' You will see it a thousand ways played out with direct care staff than you do with others, because they are so passionate about empowering, honoring, and innovating" (K. Roberts, personal communication, July 9, 2014).

CHAPTER 13

Potential Types of People-Focused Organizations

A growing number of businesses, mostly start-ups but also including some more established companies, are engaged in what has come to be called "social enterprise" (Yockey, 2010). The defining characteristic of social enterprises is that they aim both to make a profit, though perhaps a reduced profit, for equity investors and also to do some social good. The kinds of social good that such businesses do may vary, from narrow and focused initiatives to quite broad and vague intentions of social betterment. Three will be discussed in this chapter, employee stock ownership plans, benefit corporations (B Corps), and low-profit limited liability companies (L3Cs).

Employee Stock Ownership Plans

The phenomenon of employee-owned companies has been widespread in the United Kingdom, some parts of the European Union, the United States, Japan, and the former Eastern Bloc countries (Ben-Ner & Jones, 1995). The philosophical concept of employee stock ownership plans is that people are likely to become better stewards of all the systems of which they are a part—social, political, fiscal, cultural, and natural—as they gain a personal stake in the economic system, with the rights and responsibility that implies. Sauser (2009) proposes that the global economy will succeed when employees feel a stake in the business.

This has been exemplified by Timm Boettcher, president of Reality Works, in Eau Claire, Wisconsin. "The focus is on the people. People are the greatest asset. Otherwise companies will not succeed. Reality Works is 18 years old. It started with a strong mission focusing on societal benefit . . . Employee ownership and the drivers of employee ownership and the perspective benefits and social responsibility are the premise for recognition and reward at Reality Works. Employees are our most valued asset. The rewards [of the company, i.e., profits] should go to employees. There should be individual reward and recognition. Employees need to be part of the organization, and organizations need to view themselves as an extension of the individual employee. There are always some challenges, but the benefits outweigh the issues. Currently we are 11 percent employee owned. Our goal is to be 100 percent employee owned . . . When we have employees as large players in this space, the focus is on social impact. Employees go on to champion values in the society" (T. Boettcher, personal communication, July 17, 2014).

Leadbeater (as cited in Sauser, 2009, p.152) identified six advantages of employee ownership:

1. *Cooperation*: Employee ownership reduces conflict between workers, managers, and shareholders and promotes cooperation because they have shared interests.
2. *Productivity*: Workers with a stake in the business identify with it and voluntarily make an effort to cut costs, raise productivity, and improve quality, in part by monitoring the work of their colleagues.

3. *Patience*: Employee shareowners are more knowledgeable about the company than outside shareholders and therefore more patient. This should help protect the company from the short-term demands of the stock market.

4. *Loyalty*: Employees with a stake in the company are more committed. This is particularly more important in sectors with high labor turnover, and it is difficult to retain skilled staff who are in short supply.

5. *Flexibility*: Worker-owners recognize the case for pay flexibility as the fortunes of the company fluctuate. Pay automatically becomes more flexible if more of it is linked directly to profits.

6. *Risk taking*: Employee-owned enterprises come to understand the nature of the risks taken by the owners of capital. This helps underpin the legitimacy of shared ownership.

Such concepts are demonstrated by the employees of Reality Works in Eau Claire, Wisconsin. Timm Boettcher stated, "We strive to have a company that has open communication. We need to walk the talk, and being open to bring issues forward so they are not hidden or lost. . . . It's really accountability to do and say what you will do and then doing it. We have a solid group of people who will do what is best and right. Our six principles to achieve this are

"1. Focus on creating value.

"2. Having an annual review process.

"3. Holding everyone accountable.

"4. Creating an Ethics Committee where company process and products are brought together and marketed. Our board of directors knew that as the company grew there was a dedicated need to be top notch with a small footprint, focus on employees (wellness, opportunities for development of a healthy lifestyle). Impact on people. Focus on safety and creating a healthy work environment.

"5. Focusing on social impact—technically. We are culture committed with a product and social mission to employees and ethics. The culture committee evaluates, fosters, and improves employee ownership.

"6. Charitable giving programs that are driven by employees. Reality Works Employees give back three to twenty percent of annual profits . . . back to the community. Employees can take paid leave time to assist local organizations to achieve their mission. Charitable giving, employee engagement, leads to community engagement" (T. Boettcher, personal communication, July 17, 2014).

Sauser (2009) illustrates that employee participation is not a management style, but it can be considered a new way to manage. Participation can be a visible interaction between labor and management that allows employees access to real-time change and the impacts taking place. Here are seven ways to achieve this:

1. Explicitly adopt a set of common foundational values.
2. Create an organizational structure that shares power among several bodies, and thus limits its concentration.
3. Craft an organizational culture of character, and take active steps to maintain that culture throughout the life cycle of the employee stock ownership plan.
4. Manage using a servant leadership approach.

5. Transform the focus to win–win rather than adversarial strategies.
6. Foster a democratic approach at the micro level to create and sustain the business using self-managed work teams.
7. Recognize that every member-owner-employee of employee stock ownership plans must serve as a guardian of the foundational values of the organization (Sauser, 2009, p. 153).

In employee stock ownership organizational cultures, positive moral values are ingrained throughout the organization so that all of its members strive without fail to know what's right, value what's right, and do what's right. Organizations with character not only *comply* with legal and ethical standards, they also internalize them from top to bottom such that every employee becomes a champion of integrity (Sauser, 2009). Sims (2005) also found that people or employee-owned cultures are truly committed to ethical conduct [and] make ethical behavior a fundamental component of their every action and business decision. Value statements and codes of ethical conduct are used as a benchmark for judging both organizational policies and employee conduct, including conduct of leadership and the company president.

Such research is put into action as stated by Timm Boettcher:

> We know who we are and diversity of thought is number one. We strive for diverse thought in all decision-making capacity. We know this can be perceived differently with society impact. Examples of this are bringing in customer advisory groups, having a diverse supplier, diverse international distribution base differentiates us. [We practice] healthy and diverse thinking and [are] developing

a thinking process for how [the] organization will accept new thoughts and ideas, which drives the change process.

To achieve this, we have the following infrastructure in place:

- A strong safety committee. All employees [are] involved [in] how we maintain a safe and healthy work environment. We conduct plant walkthroughs.
- Conduct company social accountability audits. At this time we are doing this in 90 countries. We use the SE 8000 Process that evaluates core suppliers [for] ethical business practices, child labor, etc.
- Environmental.
- Supply base.
- Recycling. [We use a] recycle process and . . . we truly look at our footprint.
- Massive safety testing of products.
- Being responsible corporate citizens and understanding the life cycle of products and their impact.

Remember: Replication is easy. Invention is hard. (T. Boettcher, personal communication, July 17, 2014)

In essence, employee stock ownership plans create a culture that contributes to superior performance because employees have ownership in the organization. They are sustained by participatory management, financial transparency, information sharing, communication, and autonomy. Employee stock ownership plans focus on value creation and desire for greater good to make the organization successful. As a result, a pattern of strategic flexibility emerges that allows for shared risk taking and successful group goal attainment (Thompson, Shanley, & McWilliams, 2013). This creates a cooperative, participative, and people-focused culture that instills trust, creates pride in one's work, and allows for competitive advantage in the marketplace. This is explained by Lori Feiten, executive assistant to Bob Cervenka, when he was founder and owner of Phillips Plastics. Lori stated, "Employees were proud to work at Phillips Plastics. They were treated well and paid well. Bob and Debbie treated everyone like family. . . . Senior management would roll up their sleeves and help work side by side with employees. . . . If we had more business, then we were more competitive. Investing in people, equipment, and capacity helped us be more competitive in the market. We were not always the cheapest, but we had very high quality which was cheaper in the long term" (L. Feiten, personal communication, July 17, 2014).

Benefit Corporations (B Corporations)

Another type of people-oriented organization is the B Corporation, or benefit corporation. The core purpose of a B Corp is to ensure their goods and services benefit society as they continue to return profits to their shareholders (Kelly, 2009). The purpose must be the creation of a "general public benefit" (Clark & Babson, 2012). B Corporations actively include the voice of multiple stakeholders and regard themselves as living systems that deliver social benefits as a core purpose, not an incidental by-product (Kelly, 2009). In practice, the Certified B Corporation is formed as a standard for-profit corporation under state law, but then undergoes certain procedures to obtain certification from B Lab. The *benefit corporation* is a legal status in states that recognize it as a legal business under the Model Benefit Corporation Legislation (MBCL) B Lab (Clark & Babson, 2012).

A number of states have adopted benefit corporation laws, with more considering them. Though there are significant variations in detail, all benefit corporation statutes have several main elements in common. These include a provision that corporate purpose must involve pursuing other interests beyond shareholder wealth maximization, promulgation of fiduciary duties and enforcement provisions to require pursuit of that broader purpose, and a requirement for a regular (generally annual) report on how the company has pursued that broader purpose.

Benefit corporations must contain a provision in their articles, certificate of incorporation, or charter stating that they are a benefit corporation. One of the main needs for social enterprises is to find credible ways of pursuing goals beyond maximizing shareholder wealth. In essence, shareholders contract with the benefit corporation to replace the goal of shareholder wealth with the goal of pursuing or creating a general public benefit (McDonnell, 2014). The structure of a benefit corporation provides two methods of enforcement of the benefit purpose. First, as in a business corporation, shareholders maintain control through voting power. The second method of enforcement is any shareholder can bring a benefit enforcement proceeding. The benefit corporation statutes have two basic strategies for helping companies commit: reporting and duty. The first strategy uses public disclosure. In most states the report must be annual. The statutes differ somewhat in the detail required in the reports, but they generally require that a company prepare its report using an independent third party (McDonnell, 2014).

Blount and Offei-Danso (2013) have identified the seven components or services of a public benefit corporation. These are as follows:

1. Providing low-income or underserved individuals or communities with beneficial products or services;
2. Promoting economic opportunity for individuals or communities beyond the creation of jobs in the ordinary course of business;
3. Protecting or restoring the environment;
4. Improving human health;
5. Promoting the arts, sciences, or the advancement of knowledge;
6. Increasing the flow of capital to entities with a purpose to benefit society or the environment; and
7. Conferring any other particular benefit on society or the environment (p. 628).

The other statutory commitment strategy is fiduciary duty. The majority of corporations state that in most circumstances directors and officers *may* pursue objectives beyond maximizing shareholder wealth. However, under the benefit corporation statutes, firms are required to pursue the general or specific public benefits as described earlier. Failure to do so may constitute a violation of fiduciary duty and may leave the directors, officers, or corporation subject to legal violations.

Examples of the need and premise of benefit corporations are stated by Kelly (2009) in "Not Just for Profit." Richard Nelson, an economics professor at Columbia University who cofounded the field of evolutionary economics, observes that social systems evolve because of two kinds of innovation: advances in physical technologies (such as new environmental and energy technologies), and advances in social technologies (such as new forms of organization). As these two types of innovation influence each other, the governance models that emerge, such as microfinance-related structures, take their place alongside older, more established alternative models, such as cooperatives, employee-owned firms, and government-sponsored enterprises. These designs can be thought of as an emergent, new organizational species, occupying a new sector of society that is a greenhouse of design experimentation in which the future of our economy may be growing (p. 11).

B Corporations are starting a global movement to redefine what success means in business. B Corporations are certified by the non-profit B Lab to meet rigorous standards of social and environmental performance, accountability, and transparency. Certified B Corps distinguish themselves in the marketplace by voluntarily meeting higher standards and offering a positive and responsible way to do business.

B Corps translate ideas into action by creating higher quality jobs that improve the quality of life in their communities, and create value for society, not just shareholders (McDonnell, 2014). B Corps inspire greater economic opportunity, and establish themselves as leaders when addressing challenging environmental problems, while offering a workplace environment where people find fulfillment and are encouraged to bring their whole selves to work.

Low-Profit Limited Liability Company (L3C)

The third type of people-focused organization is the low-profit limited liability company (L3C). The L3C is a branch of the limited liability company (LLC) and is a low-profit entity structure that allows for philanthropic entities to invest in a company similar to an angel investor (Kucher, 2012). The L3C is a hybrid not-for-profit/

for-profit entity and is taxed as any other for-profit business. It is more commonly considered a for-profit start-up nonprofit organization. The L3C structure is an attempt at creating a method for investment in companies that do charitable work that can provide some small return to investors (Furick, 2013). This type of organization was created as a result of the 2008 global economic downturn in an effort to assist and sustain nonprofit organizations that had been significantly impacted. The uniqueness of this structure is that the not for profit can both accomplish its charitable mission and be self-sufficient by attracting outside investments and generating a positive cash flow. Social enterprises have a lot of attractions.

In essence, L3Cs allow entrepreneurs, investors, customers, and employees to do good while still doing well. They can advance some objectives that are morally attractive, while still earning a profit (entrepreneurs and investors), earning a decent wage (employees), and/or buying a useful good or service (customers). A core problem is that for some decisions, increasing profit and advancing the enterprise's stated social goods may conflict (McDonnell, 2014). There may be tradeoffs to be made, but who will make those tradeoffs, and how they should make them are the questions L3Cs face. Monitoring of management and punishment of behavior that violates the promised mix of profit and doing good may be difficult and costly.

In addition, the L3C status allows firms to pursue any legal purpose, with whatever mix of for-profit and nonprofit goals they choose. This also provides great flexibility in management structure, scope of fiduciary duty, financial structure, and exit rights. L3Cs were created to help encourage "program related investments" by charities along with investments by for-profit investors. However, the very flexibility of LLCs may present some problems. Designing a detailed set of rules

to fit the needs of a specific enterprise with such flexibilities and com-
plexities in structure may require extensive legal representation, and
much uncertainty may surround this type of organizational structure,
which utilizes business processes that have not been tested by prior
experience or by traditional methods (McDonnell, 2014).

CHAPTER 14

The Future of People-Process Cultures

Companies with a thriving people-process culture care about their communities. Such organizations recognize that strong local and regional communities help nurture a people-process culture within the organization. In a people-process culture, leadership at all levels must understand, believe, practice, and reinforce the core values. This daily practice at the individual and team levels builds and maintains the culture. Corporate culture is the best tool to enhance organizational commitment (Yukl, 2006). This commitment to the organization's core values is related to economic concepts and the efficiency of the leadership and management of the organization because people-process cultures focus on their employees as the engines of the organization. Yukl (2006) also found that strategic leadership in an organization directly or indirectly determined the organization's structure, its organizational culture and climate, and its communications. These types of leadership affect communication and influence on employees within the organization. Such leadership behaviors drive communication and public relations outcomes such as perceived organizational reputation and quality relationships (Dowling, 2004; Men, 2011).

People-process culture companies value respect for people integrated with informational transparency. The organization's commitment is enhanced because there is a strong belief and acceptance of the values and goals of the organization, a willingness to undertake substantial efforts (by the leadership) on behalf of the organization, a strong desire to stay in the organization, and a commitment to the beliefs of the organization (Ortega-Parra & Sastre-Castillo, 2013). These people-process culture companies display the following seven core values: These companies are

1. customer focused,
2. results oriented,
3. innovative,
4. respectful of people,
5. transparent,
6. ethical, and
7. socially responsible (Ortega-Parra & Sastre-Castillo, 2013).

HR practices are critical for a people-process culture to support the infrastructure of business operations by using meaningful reward and recognition systems, with performance evaluation systems tied to the business, training, and talent development. It is more than ever necessary to use individual knowledge and experience for understanding customers, designing good business processes, and making good decisions. Making use of individual knowledge for corporate interests is based on a give-and-take relationship (Pook, 2011). HR professionals in people-process cultures are astutely aware and drive such process integration and branding. Research has shown a clear link among excellence in HR strategy and organization, awareness of the challenges of demographic change, and attractiveness of the employer. The most prominent aspect of such people-process culture–focused HR strategies is the consistent implementation of business-oriented measures (Pook, 2011). Bringing employees together to work actively on strategic topics, and their implementation, establishes mechanisms that aim at continuous improvement, incorporating the solutions generated by employees, thus revealing a great potential to move from imposition to actively living change and development.

Succession Planning and Leader Development

Organizational leadership influences employees' attitudes and behavior through empowering them. Employee empowerment refers to the process or state that can be characterized as competency or "skill": and the ability to make decisions and act accordingly (Men & Stacks, 2013). Empowerment has been found to facilitate and embed the relationship between leadership and employee attitudes, specifically, job satisfaction and affective commitment to the organization (Men & Stacks, 2013).

Leadership development follows a road map. Most executives seek out smart, aggressive people, paying more attention to their accomplishments than to other critical competencies, such as people skills and emotional maturity. Yet, quick promoting of "A" performers may actually risk their careers. It is one thing to understand the importance of engaging and retaining high talent; it is another matter entirely to develop a full range of leadership competencies to ensure their success in the future. A failed executive imposes more cost to a company than the leaving of a so-called "A" performer.

Knowing how people develop certainly helps organizations in designing their succession system and leadership development pipeline (Dai, Tang, & De Meuse, 2011). By identifying the crucial leadership competencies for different position levels and matching these competencies with the right developmental experiences, organizations can reduce the time needed to prepare an individual for various leadership roles and positions, because there is little or no wasted effort on jobs that duplicate skills. However, organizations are facing increasing challenges in developing the full range of leadership competencies through traditional career ladder career experience. Developmental job assignments do not have to be formal and hierarchical and can be accomplished without moving people into new jobs but instead using lateral assignments. The direct implication of this finding is that organizations should develop their leaders early leveraging the daily operations of the business (Dai et al., 2011). Organizations therefore should focus their leadership development efforts on early assessment and identification of leadership talent potential accurately, start the development early, and assign the right experiences to develop the right competencies at the right time (Dai et al., 2011).

People-process cultures focus on helping all employees and prospective supervisors and managers develop and advance to their full potential every day in the daily operations of the business. This people-centered approach, fostered by Bob Cervenka, has cultivated the creation and development of a new generation of leaders and CEOs. This is best described by Jeffrey Cernohous, president of Interfacial Solutions: "Bob looked at me and he asked me one question. He asked me Jeff, why did you leave your company? I said at its core there were a lot of reasons, but at the core it was the way that they were applying Six Sigma processes on the R&D process . . . Then he got up and was walking out of the conference and he said how about I fund time and materials for an equity stake in your company . . . But eventually in a couple of months, Interfacial Solutions was migrated into the tech center and was incubated by Bob. One of the first things that I recognized after getting to know Phillips and the culture a little bit, the whole concept of a people-process culture resonated with me. As I had the opportunity, even though I was working on this particular business, I was able to wander some of Bob's plants. To see things like all people are important and people working together achieve more. It had a tangible impact on my personal beliefs and growth as a future leader of a company" (J. Cernohous, personal communication, July 25, 2014).

Culture matters. Not only does culture reside within us individuals, but it is also the hidden force that divides most of our behavior both inside and outside organizations (Schein, 2004). The essence of culture is not what is visible on the surface. It is the shared ways groups of people understand and interpret the world. People-process culture organizations and the leadership of people-process culture organizations understand, embrace, and leverage the people focus as a means for cultural and business success (Tidor & Morar, 2013).

Collins and Porras (2000) found that organizational culture always refers to a system of shared meaning held by members of society that can distinguish one organization from other organizations. Employees believe that these shared meanings are a set of key characteristics or "core values." A people-process culture focuses on the following core values to distinguish it from a more traditional type of organization. These core values are summarized as follows:

1. Innovation and risk taking characterizing the degree to which employees are encouraged to be innovative and take risks in their jobs;
2. Attention to detail where employees are expected to demonstrate analytical and critical thinking skills;
3. Outcome focus refers to the degree to which management focuses on results or outcomes rather than on the processes used to achieve those outcomes;

4. People orientation focused on how leadership decisions take into consideration the people within the organization and their contributions;

5. Team focus where the work activities are organized around teams rather than individuals (Swathi, Reddy, & Reddy, 2014).

Employees want their good work to be acknowledged and appreciated, with more than just money (Swathi et al., 2014). A supportive culture exhibits teamwork and a people-oriented, encouraging, trusting work environment. In these places, people are generally friendly, fair, and helpful to each other. Supportive cultures are characterized as open, harmonious, trusting, safe, equitable, sociable, relationship oriented, humanistic, collaborative, and likened to an extended family. In such a culture, employees support one another through encouraging and recognizing individuals and team contributions and accomplishments. This helps create an environment where employees in a team feel that their input is valued and appreciated. By actively participating in a team and feeling supported, team members are more likely to work cooperatively and develop a sense of shared responsibility for team outcomes (Kirkman & Rosen, 1999). This sense of trust is demonstrated by Jay Kirihara, of Farley Sales Group: "One of our mantras as a group is 'you trust first,' because, if you don't trust, the customer or somebody at the plant, nothing is going to happen. So you have to put yourself out there. So, trust that they are telling you the truth, trust that they are doing their best. Trust that first. That opens the window of understanding, then you can really develop some respect, but you have to trust first. It has to be earned too. It's like we have to earn it, but you automatically believe/trust that person" (J. Kirihara, personal communication, July 23, 2014).

Therefore, a supportive culture facilitates shared leadership in an organization (Erkutlu, 2012). People-process cultures are fully aware that by their sole focus on employees as the greatest asset of the company, communication, transparency, trust, HR, and talent development practices facilitate the foundation for supportive culture and shared leadership practices, which increase organizational trust, resiliency, productivity, and profitability. This is exemplified by Jeffrey Cernohous, president and CEO of Interfacial Solutions, "The way that leaders champion is really by showing their people that they really, truly believe and act under those core values. They are not just sitting up there at a quarterly meeting saying that these are their values. It has to happen every day. People know if you're walking the [talk]. So it's really pretty simple. To build it into your corporate DNA the leaders have to live it every day. They can't just get up in front a meeting and put on a face" (J. Cernohous, personal communication, July 25, 2014).

How to Grow a People-Process Culture

As this book has illustrated, a company's culture is embedded in its DNA. Culture develops and grows along with the company and is rooted in its values, beliefs, and behaviors. People are the reason organizational and business strategies succeed or fail. Culture controls and moderates employee perception and behavior across the entire workforce. When things are going well, organizational leaders may not consider why or how culture plays a role. It's often only when things are not working or when differences in cultures surface—such as in mergers and acquisitions—that culture becomes a consideration. The following strategies are recommended to ensure the sustainability of people-focused cultures.

Aligned Team Members

They need to be in agreement on the what, why, and how of the culture and business processes.

Focus on the People Processes

These include hiring practices, rewards, norms around new practices, and how decisions are made, etc. The recommendation is to be focused on how to retain and recruit talent.

Change Behaviors and Culture Symbols

Communicate, educate, and reinforce the how, what, why, and what the culture looks like in terms of everyday work behaviors (Eaton & Kilby, 2015).

Leaders of people-process culture organizations are astutely aware of this and leverage the "people first," "together we achieve more," and "all people benefit" core values in daily operations as well as in long-term operational strategy.

Leaders can inspire and motivate employees by clearly articulating a promising and compelling vision for the future. Empowerment is also an incentive system to reward employee performance (Charran, 2005; Gratton, Hope-Hailey, Stiles, & Truss, 1999). By empowering employees, leaders can create a perception among employees that they are being taken seriously, listened to, and valued as members of the organization. A willingness to serve people's real needs helps promote their development. This includes respect, conflict resolution, and paying attention to their legitimate interests, but also, a real appreciation for others, and acting with a sense of service and cooperation. (Men & Stacks, 2013). These are characteristics and motivators of people-process culture leaders.

Employees are the voices who represent organizations and are the formal and informal "brand" of the organization and its leadership. Favorable employee perception of the organization also helps build and protect organizational reputation in an ever-changing economic environment because employees are viewed as credible sources to external stakeholders (Grunig & Grunig, 2002; Men, 2011; White, Vanc, & Stafford, 2010). Gotsi and Wilson (2001) emphasized the role of leadership communication in creating reputation, but maintaining such organizational reputation is based on the overall evaluation of a company based on an employee's experience in the company over time. Good reputation in the eyes of employees reinforces employee commitment to the values, beliefs, mission, and objectives of the company, impacting organizational performance and effectiveness. With the advent of today's social media landscape, the employee's role as a communication asset should not be underemphasized (Men & Stacks, 2013). Employees are increasingly empowered to communicate with others and initiate dialogues within the social and public domain. How the employees perceive the organization determines what they say publicly, and their opinions consequently become the basis of organizational perception. In summary, what employees say about the organization is perceived to be more credible and authentic than messages from senior management or the communications team within the organization (Kim & Rhee, 2011).

People-process culture leaders leverage strategic communication strategies that focus on building and protecting organizational reputation while enforcing the practice of full transparency (Murray & White, 2005). Leadership behaviors—such as communicating shared vision, high performance expectations, and transparency—foster dialogue and collaboration among employees to achieve organizational goals and stimulate new perspectives and ideas while placing a high emphasis on relationships with employees, which directly influence employee perceptions of the organization. People-process culture leaders invite open communication and participation to discover employee needs and involve them in the decision-making process. People-process culture leaders and organizations focus on the core values of doing the right thing with a respect for employees and the environment. This is illustrated by commentary from Jeffrey Cernohous: "I think the clearest example is about the employees that are involved in these types of cultures. They honestly feel every day that they are making a contribution that makes a difference to their company and the world. What happens is that it almost becomes this ecosystem that prevents people that don't believe that or live those same values and to some degree filters those people out . . . When you have a culture like that [it] becomes so close knit and believes so strongly in those core values it becomes pretty apparent if there are people who are not acting that way or treating people in an appropriate way or passing blame . . . People who aren't following it [people-process culture] won't last . . . When you are in a people-based culture or a people-process culture, eventually it is self-regulating" (J. Cernohous, personal communication, July 25, 2014).

Perry (2001) suggests that the more dynamic and turbulent the economy, the higher the potential for innovation, which provides a means for people-process culture organizations to survive and remain competitive. People-process culture–based organizations use the elements of a people-process culture to leverage product innovation to gain competitive advantage, thus buffering environmental threats to survival and growth. Innovation provides a means for their competitiveness, survival, and growth. Dyer (1998) found successful firms utilized a more professional culture that focused on individuals. Zahra, Hayton, and Salvato (2004) noted that innovative products, processes, tactics, and strategies were developed more quickly and brought to market by utilizing the collective knowledge of employees. The authors determined that building relationships with external sources and suppliers also provided information, knowledge, and advice, which were critical for innovation, as well as continuous organizational learning. Creativity and innovation can be developed, sustained, and enhanced through formal and informal mechanisms such as training and education (Zahra et al., 2004).

Such knowledge generation can spark innovation and be cultivated in the following ways:

- Reinforcing trust between coworkers;
- Improving communication between staff through office and building design;
- Practicing job rotation to facilitate communication through knowledge sharing and transfer;
- Accomplishing a strong relationship between leadership decreasing hierarchical lines of communication and practicing open-door policies;
- Providing sufficient information systems;
- Providing effective rewards to reinforce knowledge;
- Increasing the level of employee participation in decision making; and
- Developing relationships with universities, technical colleges, and industry based institutes to facilitate learning and increase social capital (Al-Alawi, Al-Marzooqi, & Mohammed, 2007; Laforet, 2013).

In today's global marketplace, it is essential to work effectively with others. When leaders are asked about challenges in the workplace, relationship issues with employees tend to be the most noted concern (Brotheridge & Long, 2007). The ability to derive value from human differences is a core skill for twenty-first century leaders. Today's more global and diverse workforce requires a leader's awareness of cultural nuances and, as a result, flexible leadership focused on employees leveraging collaboration and coaching. All of these tasks require leaders to balance their own strong identity with the daily effort to understand that people (employees) are different from themselves. The concepts, testimony, and research presented in this publication illustrate that when organizations emphasize a people-process culture approach combined with social responsibility, there is a host of benefits, including more productive and satisfied employees, stronger ties to the community, and greater corporate visibility (McWilliams & Siegel, 2001). Such efforts provide needed services and support to local communities, collaboration with other organizations, establishing educational programs for potential future employees, and incorporating the needs of society into long-term corporate business goals and strategies for success (Edersheim & Wynette, 2008; Hesselbein, 2008; Vail, 2007).

References

Abu-Jarad, I.Y., Yusof, N., & Nikbin, D. (2010). A review paper on organizational culture and organizational performance. *International Journal of Business and Social Science 1*(3), 26–46.

Adler, P. S. (2001). Market, hierarchy, and trust: The knowledge economy and the future of capitalism. *Organizational Science, 12*(2), 215–234. http://pubsonline. informs.org/doi/abs/10.1287/orsc.12.2.215.10117

Al-Alawi, A. I., Al-Marzooqi, N. Y, & Mohammed, Y. F. (2007). Organizational culture and knowledge sharing: Critical success factors. *Journal of Knowledge Management, 11*(2), 22–42.

Alvesson, M. (2011). Organizational culture. Meaning, discourse, and identity. In N. Ashkanasy, C. Wilderom, & M. Peterson (Eds.), *The handbook of organizational culture and climate* (2nd ed., pp. 11–28). Los Angeles, CA: Sage.

[APA COE] American Psychological Association Center for Organizational Excellence. (2015). *Resources for employers.* Washington, DC: APA.

Argyris, C. (1993). *Knowledge for action: A guide to overcoming barriers to organizational change.* San Francisco, CA: Jossey-Bass.

Armenakis, A., Brown, S., Mehta, A. (2011). Organizational cultural: Assessment and transformation. *Journal of Change Management, 11*(3), 305–328.

Arnold, E. (2005). Managing human resources to improve employee retention. *The Health Care Manager, 24*(2), 132–140.

Bakke, D. (2013). *The decision maker.* Seattle, WA: Pear Press.

Barber, F., & Strack, R. (2005). The surprising economics of a people business. *Harvard Business Review, 6*(1), 81–90.

Bassi, L., & McMurrer, D. (2007). Maximizing your return on people. *Harvard Business Review*, March, 115–123.

Bazerman, M. H., Curhan, J. R., Moore, D. A., & Valley, K. L. (2000). Negotiation. *Annual Review of Psychology, 51*, 279–314.

Becker, B. E., Huslid, M. A., & Ulrich, D. (2001). *The HR scorecard*. Boston, MA: Harvard Business School Press.

Ben-Ner, A., & Jones, D. C. (1995). Employee participation, ownership, and productivity. A theoretical framework. *Industrial Relations, 34*(4), 532–554.

Bennis, W. (1989). *Why leaders can't lead*. San Francisco, CA: Jossey-Bass.

Birt, M., Wallis, T., & Winternitz, G. (2004). Talent retention in a changing workplace: An investigation of variables considered important to South African talent. *South African Journal of Business Management, 35*(2), 25–31.

Blanchard, K. (1999). *The Heart of the Leader: Insights on the Art of Influence*. Tulsa, OK: Honor Books.

Block, P. (1993). *Stewardship*. San Francisco, CA: Berrett-Koehler.

Blount, J., & Offei-Danso, K. (2013). The benefit corporation: A questionable solution to a non-existent problem. *St. Mary's Law Journal, 44*(3), 617–670.

Boudreau, J. W., & Ramstad, P. M. (2005). Talent ship, talent segmentation, and sustainability. A new HR decision science paradigm for a new strategy definition. *Human Resource Management, 44*, 129–136.

Brackett, M. A., Rivers, S. E., & Salovey, P. (2011). Emotional intelligence: Implications for personal, social, academic, and workplace success. *Social and Personality Compass, 5*(1), 88–103.

Brett, B., Gulliya, T., & Crispo, A. W. (2012). Emotional intelligence and organizational culture. *Insights into a Changing World Journal, 1*, 52–64.

Brotheridge, C. M., & Long, S. (2007). The real-world challenges of managers: Implications for management education. *Journal of Management Development, 26*(9), 832–842.

Cameron, K., Dutton, J., Quinn, R., & Spreitzer, G. (2005). "What is positive organizational scholarship?" Ann Arbor, MI: Ross School of Business, Michigan University, available at www.bus.umich.edu/Positive/WhatisPOS/

Cameron, K. M. & Quinn, R. E. (1999). *Diagnosing and changing organizational culture: Based on the competing values framework*. San Francisco, CA: Jossey-Bass.

Campbell, J. P., Dunnette, M. D., Lawler, E. E., & Weick, K. E. (1970). *Managerial Behaviour Performance and Effectiveness*. New York: McGraw-Hill.

Cardador, M. T., & Rupp, D. E. (2011). Organizational culture, multiple needs and the meaningfulness of work. In N. Ashkanasy, C. Wilderom, & M. Peterson (Eds.), *The handbook of organizational culture and climate* (2nd ed., pp. 158–180). Los Angeles, CA: Sage.

Champion-Hughes, R. (2001). Totally integrated employee benefits. *Public Personnel Management, 3*(3), 287–303.

Charran, R. (2005). Ending the CEO succession crisis. *Harvard Business Review, 83*(2), 72–81.

Chen, Y., Wang, W. C., & Chu, Y. C. (2010). Structural investigation of the relationship between working satisfaction factors and employee turnover. *Journal of Human Resources and Adult Learning, 6*(1), 41–50.

Ciarrochi, J., Forgas, J. P., & Mayer, J. D. (2001). *Emotional intelligence in everyday life: A scientific inquiry.* Philadelphia, PA: Psychology Press.

Clark, W. H., Jr., & Babson, E. K. (2012, December 21). *Model Benefit Corporation Legislation,* at 104(b). Retrieved from http://benefitcorp.net

Clercq, S. D., Fontaine, J. R., Anseel, F. (2008). In search of a comprehensive value model for assessing supplementary person-organization fit. *The Journal of Psychology, 142*(3), 277–302.

Colligan, M., Pennebaker, J. W., & Murphy, L. R. (1982). *Mass psychogenic illness: A social psychological analysis.* Hillsdale, NJ: Erlbaum.

Collins, J. C., & Porras, J. I. (2000). *Built to last: Successful habits of visionary companies* (3rd ed.). London: Random House Business Books.

Connell, J. (2001). Influence of firm size on organizational culture and employee morale. *Journal of Management Research, 1*(4), 220–232.

Cooke, R. A., & Hartman, J. A. (1989). Interpreting the cultural styles measured by the OCI. In *Organizational Culture Inventory. Leaders Guide.* Plymouth, MI: Human Synergistics, 23–48.

Dai, G., Tang, K. Y., & De Meuse, K. P. (2011). Leadership competencies across organizational levels: A test of the pipeline model. *Journal of Management Development, 30*(4), 366–380.

Dearlove, D., & Coomber, S. (1999). *Heart and soul and millennial values.* Skillman, NJ: Blessing/White.

De Dreu, C. K. W., Koole, S. L., & Steinel, W. (2000). Unfixing the fixed pie: A motivated information-processing approach to interactive negotiation. *Journal of Personality and Social Psychology, 79,* 975–987.

De Geus, A. (1997). *The living company: Habits for survival in a turbulent business environment.* Boston, MA: Harvard Business School Press.

Denison, D. R. (1990). *Corporate culture and organizational effectiveness*. New York: Wiley.

Denton, D. K. (1996). Creating high performance work practices. *Production and Inventory Management Journal, 37*(3), 81–85.

Dowling, G. R. (2004). Journalists' evaluation of corporate reputation, *Corporate Reputation Review, 7*(2), 196–205.

Driscoll, D. M., & Hoffman, W. M. (2000). *Ethics matters. How to implement values-driven management*. Waltham, MA: Bentley College.

Driskill, G. W. & Brenton, A.L. (2011). Identifying cultural elements. In G. W. Driskill, & A. L. Brenton, *Organizational culture in action. A cultural analysis workbook* (2nd ed., pp. 39–62). Thousand Oaks, CA: Sage.

Duxbury, L., & Gover, L. (2011). Exploring the link between organizational culture and work-family conflict. In N. Ashkanasy, C. Wilderom, & M. Peterson (Eds.), *The handbook of organizational culture and climate* (2nd ed., pp. 271–289). Los Angeles, CA: Sage.

Dyer, W. G., Jr. (1998). Culture and continuity in family firms. *Family Business Review 1*(1), 37–50.

Eaton, D., & Kilby, G. (2015). Does your organizational culture support your business strategy? *The Journal for Quality and Participation, 37*(4), 4–7.

Echols, M. E. (2007). Learning's role in talent management. *Chief Learning Officer, 6*(10), 36–40.

Edersheim, E. H., & Wynette, C. (2008). The next management revolution: Investing in social assets, *Leader to Leader, 49*, 41–48.

Emery, M. (1993). *Participative design for participative democracy*. Canberra: Center for Continuing Education. Australian National University.

Erb, M. (2011). *Inspiring employees to act as brand advocates: Insights from Herman Miller*. San Francisco, CA: Great Place to Work Institute.

Erkutlu, H. (2012). The impact of organizational culture on the relationship between shared leadership and team productivity. *Team Performance Management, 18*(1/2), 102–119.

Fichman, M. (2003). Straining towards trust: Some constraints on study trust in organizations. *Journal of Organizational Behavior, 24*(2), 133–157.

Flavel, R. W., & Williams, J. (1996). *Strategic management: A practical approach*. Sydney: Prentice Hall.

Fleming, M. (2001). *What is a safety culture?* London: Health and Safety Executive.

Forehand, G. A. & Gilmer, B. (1964). Environmental variation in studies of organizational behavior. *Psychological Bulletin, 62*(1), 361–382.

Frank, F., Finnegan, R., & Taylor, C. (2004). The race for talent: Retaining and engaging workers in the 21st century. *Human Resource Planning, 27*(3), 12–26.

Freiling, J., & Fichtner, H. (2010). Organizational culture as the glue between people and organization: A competence-based view on learning and competence building. *German Journal of Research in Human Resource Management, 24*(2), 152–172.

Fulmer, I. S., Gerhart, B., & Scott, K. S. (2003). Are the 100 best better? An empirical investigation of the relationship between being a "great place to work" and firm performance. *Personnel Psychology, 56*, 965–993.

Furick, M. T. (2013). New business structure could improve non-profits. *The Journal of Global Business Management, 9*(1), 64–70.

Galperin, B. L. (2002). *Determinants of deviance in the workplace: An empirical examination of Canada and Mexico* (Unpublished doctoral dissertation). Concordia University, Montreal, Canada.

Garratt, B. (1995). Helicopters and rotting fish: Developing strategic thinking and new roles for direction-givers. In B. Garratt (Ed.), *Developing strategic thought: Rediscovering the art of direction-giving*. London: McGraw-Hill.

Gehman, J., & Trevino, L. K. (2013). Values work: A process study of the emergence and performance of organizational values practices. *Academy of Management Journal, 6*(1), 84–112.

Giberson, T. R., Resick, C. J., Dickson, M. W., Mitchelson, J. K., Randall, K. R., & Clark, M. A. (2009). Leadership and organizational culture: Linking CEO characteristics to cultural values. *Journal of Business Psychology, 24*, 123–137.

Gladwell, M. (2000). *The tipping point: How little things can make a big difference*. New York: Little, Brown.

Goleman, D. (2001). An EI theory of performance. In C. Cherniss & D. Goleman (Eds.), *The emotionally intelligent workplace. How to select for, measure, and improve emotional intelligence in individuals, groups, and organizations* (pp. 27–44). San Francisco, CA: Jossey-Bass.

Gotsi, M., & Wilson, A. M. (2001). Corporate reputation: seeking a definition. *Corporate Communications, 6*(1), 24–30.

Govaerts, N., Kyndt, E., Dochy, F., & Baet, H. (2011). Influence of learning and working climate on the retention of talented employees. *Journal of Workplace Learning, 23*(1), 35–55.

Gratton, L., Hope-Hailey, V., Stiles, P., & Truss, C. (1999). Linking individual performance to business strategy: The people process model. *Human Resource Management, 38*(1), 17–31.

Greening, D. W., & Turban, D. B. (2000). Corporate social performance as a competitive advantage in attracting a quality workforce. *Business and Society, 39*, 254–280.

Grisez, G., & Shaw, R. (1998). *Beyond the new morality. The responsibility of freedom.* Notre Dame, IN: University of Notre Dame Press.

Grojean, M. W., Resick, C. J., Dickson, D., & Smith, B. (2004). Leaders, values, and organizational climate: Examining strategies for establishing an organizational climate regarding ethics. *Journal of Business Ethics, 55*(3), 223–241.

Grunig, J. E., & Grunig, L. A. (2002). Implications of the IABC excellence study for PR education. *Journal of Communication Management, 7*(1), 34–42.

Hara, N., & Schwen, T. M., (2006). Communities of practice in workplaces: Learning as a naturally occurring event. *Performance Improvement Quarterly, 19*(2), 93–114).

Hartel, C. E. J., & Ashkanasy, N. M. (2011). Healthy human cultures as positive work environments. In N. Ashkanasy, C. Wilderom, & M. Peterson (Eds.), *The handbook of organizational culture and climate* (2nd ed., pp. 85–100). Los Angeles, CA: Sage.

Hartnell, C. A., & Walumbwa, F. O. (2011). Transformational leadership and organizational culture: Toward integrating a multilevel framework. In N. Ashkanasy, C. Wilderom, & M. Peterson (Eds.), *The handbook of organizational culture and climate* (2nd ed., pp. 225–248). Los Angeles, CA: Sage.

Hassan, A. (2007). Human resource development and organizational values. *Journal of European Industrial Training, 31*(6), 435–448.

Hennessey, J. (1998). Revitalizing government: Does leadership make the difference? *Public Administration Review, 58*(6), 522–532.

Heorhiadi, A., La Venture, K., & Conbere, J. (2014). What do organizations need to learn to become a learning organization? *The OD Practitioner, 6*(2), 5–9.

Hesselbein, F. (2008). Collaborations make a powerful difference. *Leader to Leader, 48*, 4–7.

Hill, D. A., Hill, L. A., & Thomas, R. J. (2014). Building a game-changing talent strategy. *Harvard Business Review*, January/February, 62–68.

Hofstede, G., & Hofstede, G. J. (2005). *Cultures and organizations: Software of the mind.* New York: McGraw-Hill.

Holder, R. (1994). What America does right. Learning from companies that put people first. *Journal for Quality and Participation, 17*(6), 60–62.

Huang, H. J., & Dastmalchian, A. (2006). Implications of trust and distrust for organizations: Role of customer orientation in a four-nation study. *Personnel Review, 35*(4), 361–371.

Hultman, K. (2005). Evaluating organizational values. *Organization Development Journal, 23*(4), 32–44.

Hytter, A. (2007). Retention strategies in France and Sweden. *The Irish Journal of Management, 28*(1), 59–79.

Ibarra, H., & Hansen, M. T. (2011). Are you a collaborative leader? *Harvard Business Review,* July/August, 69–74.

Jones, G. R., & George, J. M. (1998). The experience and evolution of trust: Implications for cooperation and teamwork. *Academy of Management Review, 23*(3), 531–546.

Kabasakal, H., Asugman, G., & Develioglu, K. (2006). The role of employee preferences and organizational culture in explaining e-commerce orientations. *Journal of Human Resource Management, 17,* 464–483.

Kaczka, E., & Kirk, R. (1968). Managerial climate, work groups and organizational performance. *Administrative Science Quarterly, 12,* 252–271.

Kara, A., & Zellmer-Bruhn, M. (2011). The role of organizational culture and the underlying ideologies in the success of globally distributed teams. In N. Ashkanasy, C. Wilderom, & M. Peterson (Eds.), *The handbook of organizational culture and climate* (2nd ed., pp. 538–560). Los Angeles, CA: Sage.

Kehoe, R. R., & Wright, P. M. (2013). The impact of high-performance human resource practices on employees' attitudes and behaviors. *Journal of Management, 39*(2), 365–391.

Kelly, M. (2009). Not just for profit. *Strategy+Business, 10*(1), 9–19.

Kendall, K., & Bodinson, G. (2010). The power of people in achieving performance excellence. *The Journal for Quality and Participation, 33*(2), 10–14.

Keyton, J. (2011). *Communication and organizational culture. A key to understanding work differences.* (2nd ed.). Thousand Oaks, CA: Sage.

Kim, J., & Rhee, Y. (2011). Strategic thinking about employee communication (ECB) in public relations: Testing the models of megaphoning and scouting effects in Korea. *Journal of Public Relations Research, 23*(3), 243–268.

Kirkman, B. L., Lowe, K. L., & Young, D. L. (1999). *High performance work organizations. Definitions, practice and an annotated bibliography.* Greensboro, NC: Center for Creative Leadership.

Kirkman, B. L., & Rosen, B. (1999). Beyond self-management: Antecedents and consequences of team empowerment. *Academy of Management Journal, 42*(1), 58–74.

Koppes, L. L. (2008). Facilitating an organization to embrace a work-life effectiveness culture: A practical approach. *The Psychologist-Manager Journal, 11,* 163–184.

Kotter, J., & Heskett, J. (1992). *Corporate culture and performance.* New York: Free Press.

Kouzes, J. M., & Posner, B. Z. (1995). *The leadership challenge: How to keep getting extraordinary things done in organizations.* San Francisco, CA: Jossey-Bass.

Krishnan, T. N., & Maheshwari, S. K. (2011). A reconceptualization of career systems, its dimensions, and proposed measures. *Career Development International, 16*(7), 706–732.

Krueger, C. (1994). *The people process culture handbook.* Phillips Plastics Corporation.

Kucher, J. H. (2012). Social enterprise as a means to reduce public sector deficits. *Journal of Entrepreneurship and Public Policy, 1*(2), 147–158.

Kyles, D. (2005). Managing your multigenerational workforce. *Strategic Finance,* December, 52–55.

Labedz, C. S., & Lee, J. (2011). The mental models of HR professionals as strategic partners. *Journal of Management & Organization, 17*(1), 56–76.

Laforet, S. (2013). Innovation characteristics of young and old family-owned businesses. *Journal of Small Business and Enterprise Development, 20*(1), 204–224.

Latin Trade. (2010, September/October). Leadership lessons from Great Places to Work. *Latin Trade, 18*(5), 48–50.

La Venture, K. (2013). *How the discipline of energetics fosters double-loop learning: Lessons from multiple positivistic case studies* (Doctoral dissertation). Available from ProQuest Dissertations and Theses database.

Levering, R., & Erb, M. (2011). Emerging trends in people management. *Swiss Business,* January/February, 30–32.

Lewin, K., Lippitt, R., & White, R. K. (1939). Patterns of aggressive behavior in experimentally created social climates. *Journal of Social Psychology, 10*(1), 271–301.

Lis, B. (2012). The relevance of corporate social responsibility for a sustainable human resource management: An analysis of organizational attractiveness as a determinant in employees' selection of a (potential) employer. *Management Revenue, 23*(3), 279–295.

Litwin, G. H., & Stringer, R. A. (1968). *Motivation and organizational climate.* Boston: Division of Research, Graduate School of Business Administration, Harvard University.

Lozano, J. (1998). Ethics and corporate culture. A critical perspective. *Ethical Perspectives, 5*(1), 53–70.

Luthans, F., Vogelgesang, G. R., & Lester, P. B. (2006). Developing the psychological capital of resiliency. *Human Resource Development Review, 5*(1), 25–43.

Marquardt, M. J., & Kearsley, G. (1999). *Technology-based learning: Maximizing human performance and corporate success.* Boca Raton, FL: St. Lucie Press.

Martin, J. (2005). Organizational culture. In N. Nicholson, P. G. Audia, & M. M. Pillutla (Eds.), *The Blackwell Encyclopedia of Management* (2nd ed., Vol. 11, pp. 272–278). Malden, MA: Blackwell.

Martins, E. C., & Meyer, H. W. J. (2012). Organizational and behavioral factors that influence knowledge retention. *Journal of Knowledge Management, 16*(1), 77–96.

Mayer, J. D., & Salovey, P. (1993). The intelligence of emotional intelligence. *Intelligence, 17*(4), 433–442.

McDermott, R., & O'Dell, C. (2001). Overcoming cultural barriers to sharing knowledge. *Journal of Knowledge Management, 5*(1), 76–85.

McDonnell, B. H. (2014). Committing to do good and doing well. Fiduciary duty in benefit corporations. *Fordham Journal of Corporate & Financial Law, 20*(1), 19–72.

McWilliams, A., & Siegel, D. (2001). Corporate social responsibility: A theory of the firm perspective. *Academy of Management Review, 26*(1), 117–127.

Mele, D. (2003). Organizational humanizing cultures: Do they generate social capital? *Journal of Business Ethics, 45*(1/2), 1–2.

Men, L. R. (2011). Exploring the impact of employee empowerment on organization-employee relationship. *Public Relations Review, 37*(4), 435–437.

Men, L. R., & Stacks, D. W. (2013). The impact of leadership style and employee empowerment on perceived organizational reputation. *Journal of Communication Management, 17*(2), 171–192.

Metcalf, L., & Benn, S. (2012). Leadership for sustainability: An evaluation of leadership ability. *Journal of Business Ethics, 112*(3), 369–384.

Mezirow, J. (2000). Learning to think like an adult. In J. Mezirow (Ed.), *Learning as Transformation* (pp. 3–34). San Francisco, CA: Jossey-Bass.

Miller, N. (2010). Leading workplace innovation and change: Brave new role. *T + D, 64*(6), 54–58.

Momeni, N. (2009). The relation between managers' emotional intelligence and the organizational climate they create. *Public Personnel Management, 38*(2), 35–48.

Montiel, I. (2008). Corporate social responsibility and corporate sustainability. *Organization & Environment, 21*, 245–269.

Moran, D. W., Palmer, W., & Borstorff, P. C. (2007). An exploratory analysis of the relationship between organizational culture, regional culture, casual ambiguity, and competitive advantage in the industrial setting. *Journal of International Business Research, 6*, 61–75.

Moran, E. T., & Volkwein, J. F. (1992). The cultural approach to the formation of organizational climate. *Human Relations, 45*(1), 19–47.

Murray, K., & White, J. (2005). CEOs' views on reputation management. *Journal of Communication Management, 9*(4), 348–358.

Muthuveloo, R., & Teoh, A. P. (2013). Achieving business sustainability via i-top model. *American Journal of Economics and Business Administration, 5*(1), 15–21.

Nieminen, L., Biermeier-Hanson, B., & Denison, D. R. (2013). Aligning leadership and organizational culture: The leader-culture fit framework for coaching organizational leaders. *Consulting Psychology Journal, Practice and Research, 65*(3), 177–198.

Nishii, L. H., Lepak, D. P., & Schneider, B. (2008). Employee attributions of the "why" of HR practices: Their effects on employee attitudes and behaviors, and customer satisfaction. *Personnel Psychology, 61*, 503.

Norman, S., Luthans, B., & Luthans, K. (2005). The proposed contagion effect of hopeful leaders on the resiliency of employees and organizations. *Journal of Leadership & Organisational Studies, 12*(2), 55–64.

Oakland, S., & Oakland, J. S. (2001). Current people management activities in world-class organizations. *Total Quality Management, 12*(6), 773–788.

Ogbonna, E. and Harris, L. C. (2002). Managing organizational culture. Insights from the hospitality industry. *Human Resource Management Journal, 12*, 33–53.

Olson, J. M., & Zanna, M. P. (1993). Attitudes and attitudes change. *Annual Review of Psychology, 44*, 117–154.

Organ, D. W. (1988). *Organizational citizenship behavior: The good soldier syndrome.* Lexington, MA: Lexington Books.

Ortega-Parra, A., & Sastre-Castillo, M. A. (2013). Impact of perceived corporate culture on organizational commitment. *Management Decision, 51*(5), 1071–1083.

Osborne, R. L., & Cowen, S. S. (2002). High performance companies. The distinguishing profile. *Management Decision, 40*(3), 227–231.

Ouchi, W. G. (1981). Markets, bureaucracies, and clans. *Administrative Science Quarterly, 25*, 129–141.

Owen, K., Mundy, R., Guild, W., & Guild, R. (2001). Creating and sustaining the high performance organization. *Managing Service Quality, 11*, 10–21.

Pedler, M., Burgoyne, J., & Boydell, T. (1991). *The learning company: A strategy for sustainable development* (2nd ed.). London: McGraw-Hill.

Perry, P. M. (2001). Holding your top talent. *Research Technology Management, 44*(3), 26–30.

Pfeffer, J. (1996). *Competitive advantage through people: Unleashing the power of the work force.* Boston, MA: Harvard Business School Press.

Pfeffer, J. (1998). *The human equation: Building profits by putting people first.* Boston, MA: Harvard Business School Press.

Pfeffer, J. (2005). Changing mental models: HR's most important task. *Human Resource Management, 44*(2), 123–128.

Pfeffer, J., & Veiga, J. F. (1999). Putting people first for organizational success. *Academy of Management Executive, 13*(2), 37–40.

Phillips Plastics Corporation. (1994). *The original PPC handbook*. Phillips Plastics Corporation. Unpublished manuscript, University of Wisconsin–Stout.

Pinos, V., Twigg, N. W., Parayitam, S., & Olson, B. (2006). Leadership in the 21st century: The effect of emotional intelligence. *Academy of Strategic Management Journal*. http://www.thefreelibrary.com/Leadership+in+the+21st+century%3a+the+effect+of+emotional+intelligence.-a0166751821

Pook, K. (2011). Getting people involved. The benefit of intellectual capital management for addressing HR challenges. *Journal of European Industrial Training, 35*(6), 558–572.

Posthuma, R. A., Campion, M. C., Masimova, M. M., & Campion, M. A. (2013). A high performance work practices taxonomy: Integrating the literature and directing future research. *Journal of Management, 39*(5), 1184–1220.

Reichers, A. E., & Schneider, B. (1990). Climate and culture: An evolution of constructs. In B. Schneider (Ed.), *Organizational Climate and Culture* (pp. 1–39). San Francisco, CA: Jossey-Bass.

Repetti, R. L. (1987). Individual and common components of the social environment at work and psychological well-being. *Journal of Personality and Social Psychology, 52*(4), 710–720.

Ricks, J. M., & Williams, J. A. (2005). Strategic corporate philanthropy: Addressing frontline talent needs through an educational giving program. *Journal of Business Ethics, 60*(2), 147–157.

Robbins, S. P. (2013). *The truth about managing people*. Upper Saddle River, NJ: Pearson Education.

Rodriguez, R. (2008). Learning's impact on talent flow. *Chief Learning Officer, 7*(4), 50–64.

Rokeach, M. (1973). *The nature of human values*. New York, NY: The Free Press.

Romero, E. J. (2004). Are the great places to work also great performers? *Academy of Management Review, 18*(2), 150–152.

Roome, N. (1992). Developing environmental management systems. *Business Strategy and the Environment, 1*(1), 11–24.

Rosen, N., Greenhalgh, L., & Anderson, J. C. (1981). The cognitive structure of industrial/labor relationships. *Applied Psychology: An International Review, 30*, 217–233. doi:10.1111/j.1464-0597.1981.tb00139.x.

Rosete, D., & Ciarrochi, J. (2005). Emotional intelligence and its relationship to workplace performance outcomes of leadership effectiveness. *Leadership & Organization Development Journal, 26*(5/6), 388–399.

Russell, S. V., Haigh, N., & Griffiths, A. (2007). Understanding corporate sustainability: Recognizing the impact of different governance systems. In. S. Benn & D. Dunphy (Eds.). *Corporate governance and sustainability* (pp. 36–56). Abington: Routledge.

Russell, S. V., & McIntosh, M. (2011). Changing organizational culture for sustainability. In N. Ashkanasy, C. Wilderom, & M. Peterson (Eds.), *The handbook of organizational culture and climate* (2nd ed., pp. 393–411). Los Angeles, CA: Sage.

Sagiv, L., & Schwartz, S. H. (2000). Value priorities and subjective well-being: Direct relations and congruity effects. *European Journal of Social Psychology, 20*, 177–198.

Sagiv, L., Schwartz, S. H., & Arieli, S. (2011). Personal values, national culture, and organizations. In N. Ashkanasy, C. Wilderom, & M. Peterson (Eds.), *The handbook of organizational culture and climate* (2nd ed., pp. 515–537). Los Angeles, CA: Sage.

Sauser, W., Jr. (2009). Sustaining employee owned companies. Seven recommendations. *Journal of Business Ethics, 84*(2), 151–164.

Saylor Foundation. (2015). *Organizational behavior.* Washington, DC: Author. Retrieved from http://www.saylor.org/site/textbooks/Organizational%20 Behavior.pdf

Scaringella, L., & Malaeb, R. C. (2014). Contributions of talented people to knowledge management. *The Journal of Applied Business Research, 30*(3), 715–724.

Schein, E. H. (1992). *Organizational culture and leadership* (2nd ed.). San Francisco, CA: Jossey-Bass.

Schein, E. [H.] (2004). *Organizational culture and leadership* (3rd ed.). San Francisco, CA: Jossey-Bass.

Schein, E. [H.] (2010). *Organizational culture and leadership* (4th ed.). San Francisco, CA: Jossey-Bass.

Schiemann, W. A. (2007). Measuring and managing the ROI of human capital. *Cost Management, 21*(4), 5–15.

Schneider, B. (1975). Organizational climates: An essay. *Personnel Psychology, 28*(1), 447–479.

Schneider, B. (1983). Work climates: An interactionist perspective. In K. S. Cameron & D. S. Whetten, *Organizational effectiveness: A comparison of multiple models* (pp. 27–54). New York: Academic Press.

Schneider, B. (1985). Organizational behavior. *Annual Review of Psychology, 36*(1), 573–611.

Schneider, B. (1987). The people make the place. *Personnel Psychology, 40*(1), 437–453.

Schneider, B. (1996). Creating a climate and culture for sustainable organizational change. *Organizational Dynamics, 24*(4), 7–19.

Schneider, B., Brief, A. P., & Guzzo, R. A. (1996). Creating a climate and culture for sustainable organizational change. *Organizational Dynamics, 24*, 6–20.

Schoemaker, M., Nijhof, A., & Jonker, J. (2006). Human value management: The influence of the contemporary developments of corporate social responsibility and social capital on HRM. *Management Revue, 17*(4), 448–465.

Shin, S. J., & Zhou, J. (2003). Transformational leadership, conservation and creativity: Evidence from Korea. *Academy of Management Journal, 46*(6), 703–714.

Sidle, S. D. (2009). Is your organization a great place for bullies to work? *Academy of Management Perspectives, 23*(4), 89–91.

Sims, R. R. (2005). Restoring ethics consciousness to organizations and the workplace. Every contemporary leader's challenge. In R. R. Sims & S. A. Quatro (Eds.), *Leadership: Succeeding in the private, public, and not-for-profit sectors* (pp. 386–407). Armonk, NY: M. E. Sharp.

Sisodia, R., Wolfe, D., & Sheth, J. (2014). *Firms of endearment: How world-class companies profit from passion and purpose.* Upper Saddle River, NJ: Pearson Education.

Sullivan, W., Sullivan, R., & Buffton, B. (2002). Aligning individual and organizational values to support change. *Journal of Change Management, 2*(3), 247–254.

Swathi, B., Reddy, D. R., & Reddy, V. V. (2014). Impact of working conditions on employee participation and employee growth. *Review of HRM, 3*, 147–155.

Teare, R., Ingram, H., Prestoungrage, G., & Sandelands, E. (2002). High performance learning at work. *International Journal of Contemporary Hospitality Management, 14*(7), 375–381.

Thompson, P. B., Shanley, M., & McWilliams, A. (2013). Ownership and strategic adaptability. *Journal of Business Strategies, 30*(2), 145–179.

Tidor, A., & Morar, L. (2013). Changing organizational culture for enterprise performance. *Economic and Social Development Conference Proceedings*, 2nd International Scientific Conference, 1361–1368.

Towers Watson. (2014a). *2014 Talent management and rewards study: Making the most of the employment deal.* New York: Author.

Towers Watson. (2014b). *The targeted employee value proposition: Drive higher performance through key talent and differentiated rewards.* New York: Author.

Trice, H., & Beyer, J. (1993). *The cultures of work organizations.* Englewood Cliffs, NJ: Simon & Schuster.

Ulrich, D, (2008). Call for talent: What is the best solution? *Leadership Excellence, 25*(5), 17–17.

Vail, V. (2007). Corporate social responsibility: A third way? An interview with Sir Geoffrey Owen. *Global Business and Organizational Excellence, 26*(6), 18–27.

Valentino, C. L. (2004). The role of middle managers in the transmission and integration of organizational culture. *Journal of Healthcare Management, 49*(6), 393–404.

Van Marrewijk, M. (2004). The social dimension of organizations: Recent experiences with Great Places to Work assessment practices. *Journal of Business Ethics, 55*(2), 135–146.

Varma, A., Beatty, R. W., Schneir, C. E., & Ulrich, D. O. (1999). High performance work systems: Exciting discovery or passing fad? *Human Resources Planning, 22*(1), 26–37.

Verbos, A., Gerard, J., Forshey, P., Harding, C., & Miller, J. (2007). The positive ethical organization: Enacting a living of ethics and ethical organizational identity. *Journal of Business Ethics, 76*(1), 17–33.

Wainright, A. (1997). People first strategies get implemented. *Strategy & Leadership, 25*(1), 12–17.

Walker, J. W. (2001). Zero defections? *Human Resource Planning, 24*(1), 6–8.

Watkins, K. & Marsick, V. (1993). *Sculpting the learning organization: Lessons for the learning organization.* San Francisco, CA: Jossey-Bass.

Weymes, E. (2005). Organizations which make a difference: A philosophical argument for the "people focused organization." *Corporate Governance, 5*(2), 142–158.

White, C., Vanc, A., & Stafford, G. (2010). Internal communication, information satisfaction, and sense of community: The effect of personal influence. *Journal of Public Relations Research, 22*(1), 665–684.

Wilhelm, W. (2006). Learning organizations: What do they really do? *Leadership Excellence, 23*(3), 17–18.

Wilson, L. & Wilson, H. (1998). *Play to win!: Choosing growth over fear in work and life*. Austin, TX: Bard Press.

Yahyagil, M. Y. (2006). The fit between the concepts of organizational culture and climate. *Journal of Organizational Culture, Communication and Conflict, 10*(2), 77–105.

Yeo, R. K. (2005). Revisiting the roots of learning organization: A synthesis of the learning organization literature. *The Learning Organization, 12*(4), 368–382.

Yockey, J. W. (2010, February 1). *Does Social Enterprise Law Matter?* 4–10 (Univ. of Iowa Legal Studies Research Paper No. 14-06, 2014). Available from http://ssrn.com/abstra=2389024

Yukl, G. (2006). *Leadership in organizations* (6th ed.). Upper Saddle River, NJ: Prentice Hall.

Zahra, S. A., Hayton, J. C., & Salvato, C. (2004). Entrepreneurship in family vs. non-family firms: A resource-based analysis of the effect of organizational culture, *Entrepreneurship Theory and Practice, 28*(4), 363–381.

Zairi, M. (1998). Managing human resources in healthcare: Learning from world class practices. Part 1. *Health Manpower Management, 24*(2), 48–57.

Index

About the Authors

Dr. Black, Associate Professor, University of Wisconsin-Stout

www.linkedin.com/in/jeanettemblack

Dr. Jeanette Black is an Associate Professor and Endowed Chair for People Process Culture in the Department of Operations and Management, College of Management, at the University of Wisconsin-Stout, Menomonie WI. She teaches graduate courses in Organizational Development/Change Management, Organizational Culture, and Human Resource Development. She supervises many graduate student research projects in the private and nonprofit sector each semester. Dr. Black graduated from the University of St. Thomas, Minneapolis, MN, Doctoral Program in Organization Learning and Development in 2007. Her Doctoral Research investigated the lived experiences of women in their workplace relationships with supervisors and their use of Emotional Intelligence Competencies. Dr. Black has presented research on the effects of truck cab design for women truck drivers at the 2014 Women's Issues in Transportation (WIit) Conference in Paris, France. She conducts research with organizations in the private and nonprofit sectors on organizational culture, transformational change, and leadership development. Dr. Black may be reached at blackj@uwstout.edu.

Dr. Kelly La Venture

www.linkedin.com/in/kellylaventure

Dr. Kelly La Venture is Assistant Professor and Director of Marketing Assistance and Research Solutions in the
Department of Business Administration, College of Business, Technology
and Communication, at Bemidji State
University, Bemidji, MN. Dr. La Venture teaches courses in research,
management, and marketing. She graduated from the University of
St. Thomas, Minneapolis, MN, Doctoral Program in Organization
Learning and Development in 2013. Her doctoral research investigated the proposition that the application of learned skills and concepts of (1) critical reflection of self-behavior, (2) identification of
values or assumptions underlying the behavior, (3) changes in underlying values or assumptions, and (4) changes in the behavior, fosters
double-loop learning.

Dr. La Venture has presented research on double-loop learning at
the Organization Development Network (ODN) Conference in San
Jose, CA, and Socio-Economic Approach to Management (SEAM) at
the Ireland International Conference on Education (IICE) in Dublin,
Ireland. Dr. La Venture conducts research and consults with organizations in the private and nonprofit sectors. She finds the most satisfying work is helping organizations cultivate healthy and people-focused
environments. She may be reached at klaventure@bemidjistate.edu.

The University of Wisconsin-Stout Menomonie, WI

UW-Stout is a comprehensive, career-focused university where students, faculty, and staff use applied learning, scientific theory, humanistic understanding, creativity, and research to solve real-world problems, grow the state's economy, and serve society. UW-Stout provides a distinctive array of innovative programs that produce graduates who are prized in the marketplace. The six-month post-graduation employment rate for UW-Stout graduates has been at 97 percent for more than a decade, with more than three-quarters of them in their field of study. The university's nearly 9,300 students, supported by 472 faculty and instructional academic staff and 949 additional staff, can select from 45 undergraduate programs, 20 master's degree programs, and three advanced degree programs: Ed.S. in Career and Technical Education, Ed.S. in School Psychology, and Ed.D. in Career and Technical Education. The university is located on a beautiful campus in Menomonie, situated in western Wisconsin, 60 minutes east of Minneapolis-St. Paul on Interstate 94. The campus is located in the scenic Chippewa Valley Region with a population base of more than 200,000. For more information, please visit http://www.uwstout.edu/.

CPSIA information can be obtained
at www.ICGtesting.com
Printed in the USA
LVHW041935080723
751847LV00001B/76